Stephanie Ihlen

Finding Joy in God's Timing

NORTHWESTERN PUBLISHING HOUSE
Milwaukee, Wisconsin

Northwestern Publishing House
N16W23379 Stone Ridge Dr., Waukesha WI 53188-1108
www.nph.net
© 2024 by Northwestern Publishing House
Published 2024
Printed in the United States of America
ISBN 978-0-8100-2935-4
ISBN 978-0-8100-2936-1 (e-book)

24 25 26 27 28 29 30 31 32 33   10 9 8 7 6 5 4 3 2 1

Foreword

What if you were challenged to dedicate yourself to a specific pattern of thinking during a certain number of days, and under definite spiritual disciplines? Would you accept the experiment?

That's exactly what happened for several people who were invited not just to touch on a study topic like seeking God more or loving God more. They were to devote themselves to a full 180 days of reading about that topic in the Bible itself, praying about the topic for themselves, journaling their adventure, and even engaging an accountability partner to help them stick to the commitment and to talk through the details they were discovering. After that, they were to share what they learned about the topic with you.

You are looking at the results of one of the challenges.

And you're in for quite a journey. Whether you read this by yourself, with a small group of fellow inquirers, or in another setting, you will gain tremendous insights from reading what this author learned.

Do you have to do your own 180? Won't that first take a lot of scriptural knowledge? No, not at all. But if you do take up the challenge for yourself, there's no telling the spiritual growth you'll experience. After 180 days of reading and considering God's Word on a spiritual topic, your Savior promises rich dividends. "Consider carefully what you hear," he says in Mark 4:24. "With the measure you use, it will be measured to you—and even more." You will certainly discover rich understanding. You may even experience a complete turnaround in your life with Jesus!

Now read what happened when Stephanie Ihlen accepted the challenge.

Contents

Prologue

Prologue

Not going to lie, it's taken a lot to get this journal started. If I start the journal, that means I have to write in it every day for the next 6 months. Talk about commitment! But if I can check my Facebook and e-mail every day, I think I can probably make time for journaling. . . . My prayer is that HE uses me to further HIS kingdom—whether through the book I'll end up writing after the 6 months or maybe just a newfound attitude . . . or a conversation I'll get to have with someone about this "experiment." I am intrigued by this challenge if you will, but as with most things new to me I'm a bit apprehensive.
[Day 1 of 180]

Scared, intrigued, excited, and unsure where it would lead me. Those were my feelings when I was asked to be one of the authors of the My 180 series, in which each author was appointed a topic to think, pray, and journal about daily for six months straight (180 days). Then we were to write a book about our journey, the experiment, and how it had changed our lives. The fact that I said yes to this assignment surprised my husband, but I think it surprised me even more. I have never been one to journal or aspire to write a book like my more literary and creative friends. Rather, I said yes because I prayed about it, and I became convinced that this was a good way for me to become closer to God and serve him. I knew at the very least that even if this book never was published and not a soul read it, God would teach me immeasurably through this adventure.

My 180 focus was on waiting—waiting on God. Waiting on God is not simply waiting for life events; it is not waiting for God as if he might not show up. It is a matter of waiting on God by leaning on him, by recognizing his power and perfection. You will see countless times in this book how weak I can be when it comes to waiting. Whether waiting for lab results or a call from the realtor, I so easily think my timing is the right timing. I was excited for this to be my topic because I felt like it would challenge me to push myself and grow in ways that I never would have otherwise. Waiting on God doesn't come easily for me, so I was excited to stretch myself spiritually.

Thank you for embarking on this journey through my eyes and heart. God reminds his people time and time again in the Bible that he loves to use the least likely people to get his work done, like Rahab the prostitute, David the runt of the litter, or coldhearted Jonah covered in fish vomit. If you don't know these stories, or if you want to read them again, open your Bible. You can read about David being anointed king in 1 Samuel chapter 16, and Rahab's story is in Joshua chapter 2. Jonah has his own book in the Bible! You can read his prayer from the belly of the fish in Jonah chapter 2.

Sometimes if you say no to God, he pushes you to change your response to yes. During the last six months, I have laughed, cried, and been in awe of God's grace. If you have read with me this far, take a moment to prepare your heart and mind for an awesome and mysterious God to use you how he sees fit.

Dear Lord, open my heart and mind to teach me to serve and honor you and see your grace in everyday life. Please help me learn to wait on you more because your timing is the best timing. In your name, I pray. Amen.

The way I pursued this book was to write like I was sharing these experiences, thoughts, and emotions with a friend over a cup of coffee, around a campfire, or on a walk in a quiet park. These are my simple, everyday life experiences together with extra time devoted to prayer and Bible reading and what I've gleaned from them. While I expect you will know me pretty well by the end of this book, I hope that this experience helps you know Christ immeasurably more. I will challenge you, in the "Your Turn" sections, to think about the waiting on God topic and, in the "Travel Tips" sections of the book, to consider embarking on your own 180 journey.

I pray this book will challenge your perspective. It is my hope that when you see the 180-degree turn this project caused in my life, you will want to pursue a 180 of your own. If not 180 days, maybe 50? maybe 100? You may surprise yourself how quickly God can move you.

Go ahead and make yourself a cup of coffee, find your favorite spot on the couch, put a blanket on your lap, convince your spouse to go work on that never-ending house project, and have a conversation with me. I want to help you see God's hand in your daily life. I want to encourage you to realign your life to fit God's will. You will see my heartbreak over struggles in my family, my joy over family blessings, my continued passion for youth ministry, my exhaustion in working as a nurse, and my amazement at hearing a dear friend's adoption story. By focusing, praying, reading, and journaling about waiting on God's timing, I was so clearly reminded that God knows the plans he has for me (Jeremiah 29:11) and there is a time for everything (Ecclesiastes chapter 3). My 180 has taught me to wait on God to show me his grace, patience, and timing. He has also shown me his love through others. His plans are clearly worth the wait. I promise I won't fill this book with flowery language, but I will fill it with honesty. Let's have an honest chat.

My name is Stephanie Ihlen. I am a full-time nurse on an inpatient medicine/oncology unit, wife to my best friend Ben, a mom (spoiler: this was not the case at the beginning of my 180 journey), and a Jesus pursuer. I am honored to be sharing my 180 change with you.

Waiting on God Means Relying on His Control and Timing

Why Wait?

Just read with Ben the account of the fall into sin. Do you think that perfect Adam and Eve would need to be dedicated to wait on God more? [Day 8 of 180]

Ben and I were reading Genesis together as part of our daily Bible reading, and this text reframed my thoughts to focus on waiting on God more. When you read the creation account in the first two chapters of Genesis, you see that Adam and Eve were created in God's image, meaning they were sinless. As I continued to read, I thought, "Adam and Eve were perfect. Would they need to concentrate, meditate, and pray about waiting on God more?" I don't think so. They were perfect, just the way God made them. Before the fall into sin, Adam and Eve perfectly relied on God and would not have needed a 180 journey. But sin did enter the world through them. Solomon tells us in Ecclesiastes 7:29, "This only have I found: God created mankind upright, but they have gone in search of many schemes." The fact that we even need to try so hard to learn to wait on God shows that we aren't perfect like Adam and Eve were. We are "in search of many schemes."

As a sinful human being, my natural inclination is to be and feel independent. I want to feel like I can do anything without any help, but God did not create me that way. I need to be completely dependent on

God. There's nothing truly good I can do apart from him. Jesus said, "I am the vine; you are the branches. If you remain in me and I in you, you will bear much fruit; apart from me you can do nothing" (John 15:5). As a nurse, I tend to see things in medical terms. This verse reminds me of arteries. Arteries provide blood to your whole body. If you have healthy arteries, but your heart stops, the arteries will not do any good. Their source is from the beating heart; they are simply a conduit. Such is the way with people. God is the center of it all, and when we are connected to him, we display good because God is the definition of good. Because of our dependence on him and because of the evil of the world around us (it seems to be getting worse and worse), we are not able to perfectly plan anything that happens in our lives. God is in control.

Early on in my journey, I felt like my waiting on God consisted of expecting him to step in when things went awry, but I soon realized that waiting on God means so much more than that. Christians must wait for many things, but our greatest need is to wait on God: to learn to wait on his timing and for him to show his grace. This concept is hard for puny little human brains to understand because the sinful nature wants to be in control and live independently from God. What I forget to remember is that because we Christians are reliant on God, he can show us his strength. This strength is something I am thankful for. Thankful that since I cannot do anything on my own accord, I can fully appreciate and understand the sweet truth that I have a Savior who gave up his life on the cross. "For God so loved the world that he gave his one and only Son, that whoever believes in him shall not perish but have eternal life" (John 3:16). Thankful that Jesus said no to all the temptations the devil put in his way because I surely cannot (Matthew 4:1-11). Thankful that God has my life mapped out because there's no way I could have it all planned to his glory or my good.

God reminds us of our reliance on him through the apostle Paul in the Bible. Paul wasn't always an apostle or follower of Christ. In fact, he had persecuted those who were believers. We see in Acts chapter 4 that Paul had a unique awakening in which God blinded him for three days, changed his heart, and brought him to faith in Jesus. Paul spent the rest of his life traveling to many countries, encountering people of all backgrounds, and speaking the truth of Jesus. He was even imprisoned because of his Jesus-believing outreach. Paul said to the Corinthians,

> In order to keep me from becoming conceited, I was given a thorn in my flesh, a messenger of Satan, to torment me. Three times I pleaded with the Lord to take it away from me. But he said to me, "My grace is sufficient for you, for my power is made perfect in weakness." Therefore I will boast all the more gladly about my weaknesses, so that Christ's power may rest on me. That is why, for Christ's sake, I delight in weaknesses, in insults, in hardships, in persecutions, in difficulties. For when I am weak, then I am strong. (2 Corinthians 12:7-10)

It seems counterintuitive to "delight in weaknesses, in insults, in hardships, in persecutions, in difficulties." When life gets hard, I often feel like just running away or giving up. But Paul reminds me that when times get tough, I lean on God a little more and see how magnificent he really is, because life can throw some curveballs that make me feel pretty small. Paul's attitude is one I pray God gives me the strength to live out. Christians are not perfect like Adam and Eve were before they sinned. We do need to dedicate ourselves to waiting on God. Because of his grace, the same grace he extended to Paul, we can wait even when prayers appear unanswered or plans seem uprooted. Why wait? We wait on God so he can show us his perfect love and power.

Come as You Are

I did not write this book specifically for people of a certain background or demographic. Some people reading this maybe don't miss a Sunday church service and are super active with Christian outreach in their congregations. Other people reading this may go to church occasionally when they feel like it has been a while. Others reading this may not have stepped foot in a church since they were five years old—or ever for that matter.

No matter your background, anyone can begin a 180 journey. The Bible is written for all people of all time, and it is the way God directly talks with you. I can imagine it would be daunting to open a Bible for the first time or confusing if you have to come up with a Bible reading plan on your own. The internet can be a great starting point, as can a Bible with a concordance. A biblical concordance is a reference tool you can use to look up topics arranged alphabetically and find Bible passages related to those topics. Biblegateway.com is another helpful tool you can use to search biblical topics. Having located specific passages, you could then come up with a list of sections you would like to read and assign each to a week during your 180 journey. Organizing the Bible sections you want to read during your journey is beneficial for you to stay on track and not scramble at the beginning of every week trying to figure out what section you'd like to read. In general, if you are just starting out, the books in the New Testament may be the best starting point. They are a bit easier to understand and often have a straightforward correlation to everyday life. That does not mean the Old Testament books should be ignored completely, but they do take perhaps a little more thought to find a takeaway. The parts of the Bible you choose to read may depend on your level of biblical knowledge or training, but no matter what your spiritual life is like, you can embark on a 180 journey. That's what digging in the Word is—listening to what God is saying to you and applying it to your life.

The goal of the 180 journey is to see your relationship with Christ deepen or to begin your journey in Jesus if you're new to Christianity. You may even be surprised at the way God blesses you and reveals himself to you in a relatively short time.

Waiting for a Baby

"Tag, you're it!" That's the voicemail that my Lyme Nurse Practitioner left on my phone today. Of course it was a super crazy day today at work and I didn't get her voicemail until much later in the day. More waiting. More waiting on God more. [Day 26 of 180]

Still waiting on my Nurse Practitioner. Left another voicemail saying I'm off today and tomorrow. Praying she gets back to us soon, but now I'm wondering if God is saying to explore different options or to wait on her. I'll think and pray about it. Waiting is not something I'm good at when it comes to big life decisions. [Day 38 of 180]

I have been told many times, "You have so much patience." Yes, it is true I have patience with my nieces and nephews and as a nurse with my patients. But what I'm not so great at is being patient about the big-picture things in my life. I've learned that I'm certainly not patient when it comes to waiting on God.

If you were to read my many journal entries like the one above, you would notice that the topic of Lyme disease and pregnancy was heavy on my heart. I wrote on this topic a lot. I wanted a quick answer, and I was growing impatient, since this whole process took months. But God taught me the importance of waiting on him more, and he used my loving husband, Ben, to help me through it.

I wanted to get pregnant in August. It just seemed like a good time. It was at the end of all our summer vacations, and I wouldn't have to worry about morning sickness in the middle of traveling.

My husband, who can be much more practical than I (there, I said it), was a bit more cautious. He wasn't on board with my thoughts on August, and he voiced his concerns, wanting to wait a little longer. Ben had a valid reason to be cautious that I wanted to overlook. I had been treated for chronic Lyme disease for a full year. This involved taking multiple types of antibiotics. Even though it was four years later when I wanted to conceive, there still was some concern. I had been cautioned about the possible danger of becoming pregnant because there is some evidence indicating that Lyme disease can be passed on to children. The problem is that there is not nearly enough information on latent Lyme disease posttreatment. My nurse practitioner, along with many other Lyme practitioners, believe that Lyme is never fully eradicated from the body. Unfortunately, there is not a reliable way to test that the disease has been eradicated, so Lyme practitioners often base the length of antibiotic use on symptoms. The school of thought is that the antibiotics kill Lyme disease, but *borrelia* (the species name of the Lyme bacteria) is extremely intelligent and can hide in certain areas of the body and lay dormant until a stressor such as pregnancy comes along and causes the *borrelia* to reactivate and wreak havoc on the body, and maybe the unborn baby's body, in the form of dozens of symptoms.

When I had finished my treatment four years earlier, my Lyme practitioner had told me to contact her if I became pregnant. She would then put me on prophylactic antibiotics for the entirety of the pregnancy. In the back of my mind, I did remember my nurse practitioner's recommendation to contact her, but I was impatient and wanted to start trying for a baby right away in August.

I thought, "I've been feeling great the last number of years. I don't want to be on antibiotics while I'm pregnant!"

Ben's thought was "We need to do this right, Steph. I know you're against the overuse of antibiotics after taking the more natural route the last couple of years, but we need to do what's right for our baby."

I had altered my thought process when it came to my health and well-being. The yearlong affair of multi-antibiotic treatment did a number on my gut flora. My Lyme symptoms were resolved, but it left my body feeling off. I began taking heavy-duty probiotics to help restore the good bacteria that had been killed with the bad Lyme bacteria. I started taking vitamins, cod liver oil, and supplements to boost energy and restore health. I also began eating healthier and doing more reading and research on how much of an impact nutrition has on health. I cut back on gluten, dairy, and sugar. I took control of my wellness, and I slowly started to feel the positive effects of such. I do not regret taking antibiotics for my treatment, but I think the aftermath

6

taught me a ton about my body. Instead of rushing to take antibiotics like I used to, I try herbal remedies and vitamins first. It reversed my thinking on health. I also began seeing a doctor of holistic medicine in addition to my primary medical doctor, and I felt the results. I was feeling so much better after taking the recommended supplements from my holistic doctor.

After many long talks and prayers, I reluctantly agreed to contact my Lyme specialist. All I wanted was a quick phone conversation with her, since her clinic was about five hours away, to tell me yes or no to antibiotics. At the time I was working day shift at the hospital, and she always seemed to return my phone calls while I was working. Sometimes I would call back ten minutes after she had called, right after I had finished helping my patient back into bed or administering a medication, and I would get her clinic voice mail.

I journaled about the phone tag scenario often. I became frustrated, frustrated that the answers were not happening quickly enough for me. I wondered, "Doesn't God want me to have children?" However, the blessing of being on this 180 journey turned my doubts into reliance on him. The hardships in the waiting turned into blessings in the waiting.

First, I learned to appreciate the blessing of Ben caring so deeply about me and our possible future baby. He cared enough to encourage me to put the brakes on this whole process, even if I didn't want to hear it at the time. Second, I learned that God is much bigger than all the plans I sketch out for my life. He not only understands the status of my health, but he also gives the gift of health to me. For that I am earnestly thankful! I also learned that as hard as I try to fix things myself, there is nothing I can do to speed up the process God has in store for me.

I waited and looked for answers. In September, after about one month of phone tag, Ben and I decided to see if there were other Lyme practitioners in the area. I contacted the International Lyme and Associated Diseases Society website for an extremely short list of doctors in Wisconsin who treat Lyme disease. I booked the earliest appointment with the doctor closest to my home. After a couple of visits, one by myself and one with Ben, we decided not to see that provider any further.

The doctor did not seem to respect us the way we'd like and seemed dismissive of our concerns. It was time to wait again.

After much discussion and prayer about antibiotics and their possible effects on a fetus, Ben and I chose the natural route and found a good practitioner. To us this route seemed the safest for a baby. The thought is that the oral homeopathic medicines made my body more aware of the *borrelia* bacteria possibly hidden or dormant inside me and enabled my body to pinpoint the bacteria as foreign instead of as a part of me. I began this homeopathic regimen and was on it for the recommended full two months (October and November) before we started trying for a baby. More waiting, but my homeopathic practitioner felt like this two-month wait was necessary to avoid putting any extra stress on a future baby.

The first month of trying for a baby, I felt confident it would just happen. Ben and I had waited this long to start, so it made sense that God would certainly bless us right away. Right? Not exactly. My heart sank as the pregnancy test just showed one line, indicating negative. The next month I was so ready to try again. I thought, "This has to be it." But again, God was teaching me patience. I somehow came down with mononucleosis. Yes, mono. Who knows what I'm exposed to at work or even in everyday life. I was in bed for ten days and exhausted for a few weeks after I broke out of the acute stage. So I did not get pregnant that month. The following month Ben got sick with a bad cold and a sore throat.

As Ben and I entered the fourth month of trying, I felt like I had a newfound appreciation for patience. We can try so hard to make things happen in this life, but God holds the road map to it all. I prayed for God to show me how to be patient in his timing. I learned so much, but I have much more to learn. The learning didn't come all at once but, rather, gradually over time. I learned that God is ultimately in control of my health, and he has proven again and again how much he cares for me. I learned, upon further reflection, that my restlessness about getting pregnant was actually my fear that I was losing control. I learned to put that control back into God's hands. I became less anxious about the future and strangely comfortable that if and when it happened, it would be perfect timing because it would be God's timing.

Update

It took a while, but God gave us a beautiful, healthy baby boy. As I tuck him into bed each night, I can't help praising God for the gifts he gives his people!

I feel so incredibly blessed. There are many people in my life who have had miscarriages at all stages of pregnancy and some who struggle with infertility. As heartbreaking as it is to see loved ones go through those incredibly trying times, their understanding, grace, and perseverance have truly inspired me. None of us deserve to have children despite what great parents we would make or how hard we have tried. Children are completely a gift from God, and ultimately they are *his*. We have been given the opportunity to raise, teach, and watch them here on this earth, but they were never meant to live on this earth and be our children forever. No, what is most important is that they know their Savior and understand and boldly believe that they are children of God and will be in heaven someday.

Maybe you are one of those struggling people. Maybe you just found out you aren't able to have children, and it's broken your heart. But God may be opening other doors for you. Perhaps the open door is volunteering at a women's center and counseling young women to choose life, or perhaps it's starting the process for adoption. Maybe your finances crashed right before having your baby, and you find yourself relying on Jesus a ton more than you typically would have. It's funny how we plan something in life and something else completely unexpected comes into our vision. It's these events that bring us even closer to Christ and have us lean on him even more. Understanding more deeply God's timing, power, and grace makes waiting on children a more peaceful time.

Sarai and Hagar

*God promised Abram and Sarai that they would have a son, even
in their old age. They must have gotten tired waiting on God,
that they took matters into their own hands, and had Abram
sleep with their slave, Hagar to conceive. [Day 40 of 180]*

My 180 readings reminded me that I'm not the first wife to get impatient
for God to give me a child. Because I was focusing on waiting on God
more, it became easier and easier to pick up on this in my everyday life or
personal Bible study. The biblical story of Abram and Sarai and their slave
Hagar exemplified what waiting on God really means.

Abram and Sarai were married and living in the land of Canaan. God
had greatly blessed them; they had much in livestock, silver, and gold.
The Lord promised Abram that he would continue to bless him,

> I will make you into a great nation,
>   and I will bless you;
> I will make your name great,
>   and you will be a blessing.
> I will bless those who bless you,
>   and whoever curses you I will curse;
> and all peoples on earth
>   will be blessed through you. (Genesis 12:2,3)

God also promised Abram that Sarai would become pregnant and
have a son even in their old age. He told Abram to "look up at the sky
and count the stars—if indeed you can count them." Then he said to him,
"So shall your offspring be" (Genesis 15:5).

Abram and Sarai waited ten years to conceive, and they were tired of
waiting on God to make good on his promise. Sarai took matters into her
own hands and convinced Abram to sleep with her slave Hagar in order
to produce an heir (Genesis chapter 16). This may seem strange, this historical surrogate mother idea, but it was not uncommon in biblical times.
Sarai's plan did not make her happy; forgetting to wait on God usually
doesn't. Genesis 16:4 tells us how Hagar behaved: "When she knew she
was pregnant, she began to despise her mistress." Then Sarai treated Hagar

cruelly. Abram knew about his wife mistreating Hagar, but he did not correct her. Hagar then ran away, and the angel of the Lord appeared to her in the desert. The angel said to her,

> "Go back to your mistress and submit to her." The angel added, "I will increase your descendants so much that they will be too numerous to count."

> The angel of the LORD also said to her:

> "You are now pregnant
>   and you will give birth to a son.
> You shall name him Ishmael,
>   for the LORD has heard of your misery."
> (Genesis 16:9-11)

God was extremely gracious to Hagar and blessed her despite the circumstances, despite the sins of all three people. Not only did God bless Hagar, but he also was gracious to Sarai. God changed Sarai's name to Sarah: "As for Sarai your wife, you are no longer to call her Sarai; her name will be Sarah. I will bless her and will surely give you a son by her. I will bless her so that she will be the mother of nations; kings of peoples will come from her" (Genesis 17:15,16). God fulfilled his promise that one day Sarah would conceive even though she was well past her child-bearing years. God blessed her with a son named Isaac. Ishmael, Hagar's son, would have been about 14 years old when Isaac was born. Even though Sarah resented Hagar and Ishmael, God blessed the mother and son and made Ishmael into a great nation.

God had promised that the line of the Savior would come from Abram, and God blessed him and Sarah with Isaac to carry on that line. God changed Abram's name to Abraham: "No longer will you be called Abram; your name will be Abraham, for I have made you a father of many nations" (Genesis 17:5).

This story is a reminder for me. If it were one hundred percent up to us to obey God's commands and listen to him unconditionally, we would certainly fail. Abraham and Sarah were not trusting in God. They grew impatient and took the situation into their own hands instead of going to

God. Even though they did not listen to God and his promise, God was still gracious. If I stop listening and fall, God is still loving and forgiving.

Abraham and Sarah's story also shows us that God uses ordinary, sinful people to fulfill his divine plan. Even though Abraham and Sarah were impatient and did not trust in God's plan of her conceiving, God still blessed them years later with Isaac, who would become the ancestor of the Israelites, the nation from which Jesus came.

The story shows God working through tragic or difficult circumstances, which do not seem to have any good in them at all, to fulfill his will. He also works through unlikely and seemingly unfit leaders to fulfill his will. What comfort it is for us to remember that we don't need to have it all figured out because God certainly does. And what about when *we* are the ones who seem unfit, who don't have any good in us? The way God stuck with doubting Sarah and proud Hagar encourages me. He sticks with people who are bad at waiting on him. God blesses those who don't deserve it at all, and he works through those people even if they are not following his will. This means that God can work through people like me, who sometimes run in the opposite direction when they see signs that maybe God is pulling them in a way they don't want to go.

Through journaling, reflecting, praying, and reading the Bible for 180 days, I've taken greater notice of God's divine plan. Yet God has a bigger plan than I am able to see or notice fully. I've learned that he uses improbable people, circumstances, and situations to fulfill his will. He does not always use cookie-cutter, safe, inside-the-box situations and people to further his kingdom. He uses people from all backgrounds with all different philosophies and ideas. My challenge to you is to find God in the noisy, quiet, chaotic, and calm stages of life. It doesn't matter what season of life; he's there through the thick and thin. He's there through it all, and what a blessing that is. From these historical accounts it's easy to see that since the beginning of time people have not been successfully waiting on God, and I'll be the first to admit I need God's grace in this area. My prayer is to ask God to wash all my worry and doubt away, help me completely trust in Christ, and give me patience in the waiting.

YOUR TURN

- Have there been times when you didn't want to wait on God more and you took things into your own hands?

- What are some lessons God taught you during those times?

- What are some ways you could remind yourself to wait on God more instead of leaning on your own logic, wisdom, desire, etc.? Try to be specific.

Car Troubles

During my 180, I've learned how hard it is to trust God in the simple aspects of life and how easy it is to think I have it handled on my own. Instead of constantly waiting for his help or for him to act, I find myself thinking that God is on standby—as if God is the one waiting on me, waiting for me to get in over my head. I think he will jump in and out of a situation when it's convenient for me or when I feel like I need him. I learned a lesson about this pretty much in the middle of my 180 journey. Ben and I were having issues with our 2001 Jeep Grand Cherokee (Ben's pride and joy!). It had died the week before, barely getting Ben to work, and this happened on his birthday of all days. He ended up having to call a tow truck at work so the local car repair shop could fix the alternator. Exactly six days later, he got into the Jeep to head to work, and it wouldn't start. Thankfully Ben's coworker lived a mile away so Ben was able to quickly call him to see if he could jump-start the Jeep. Well, the car still wouldn't start even with a jump, so Ben's coworker ended up driving him to work.

When Ben came home that evening, he went right to work replacing the battery on the car. Let me tell you, Ben and I were both praying like crazy that it was just a $115 battery fix and not a nail in the coffin for our Jeep. At the time, we had just bought a house and were renovating and installing a wood-burning stove, which we knew full well were luxuries. We, however, preferred not to add a new (used) car to the red in our bank account. We were hoping to wait it out until summer to buy a replacement car for the Jeep! We were both feeling frustrated because this was not a part of our plans.

Ben installed the new $115 battery, and then it was the moment of truth: Would the Jeep start? We held our breath, waited, and then heard the Jeep slowly turn over. Then there was the steady, sweet, and low hum of the Jeep. We were so excited! Ben was literally running laps inside our little home celebrating. We were overjoyed. Ben took the Jeep for a test-drive around the neighborhood, and it passed with flying colors.

Since Ben was on a roll with fixing the car, I asked him to replace one of the headlights on our other car, the one I usually drive. We had known about the burned-out light, but we had been neglecting it for a week or two. When I asked Ben, he replied, "Sure, no problem."

He had never replaced this headlight before, and by this time the sun had gone down. With just the dim garage light and a headlamp, it was hard for him to see what he was doing, and the high temperature that day had been only 7 degrees. After about 45 minutes of tinkering around, he determined that I had bought the bulb for the brights, not the low beams. To top it all off, the auto parts store was closing in 20 minutes. I felt so bad about the careless mistake I had made. I wanted to make it right, so I quickly raced to the auto parts store in our now drivable Jeep (thank God!). I was worrying and feeling frustrated the whole way there, but I made it just before the open sign went off in the window. As I was reflecting on this situation sometime later, the Bible verse that came to mind was Psalm 106:13: "They soon forgot what he had done and did not wait for his plan to unfold."

Typically, when we know a task is going to be difficult or trying, we are on our knees. In our case, we were worried that the fix on the Jeep would be a high price, so we prayed. After God answered our prayers that cold winter night about a relatively inexpensive fix for the Jeep, we were praising and thanking Jesus! But when it came time to do an easy task like replacing the headlight, it was like we got amnesia and completely forgot how God had helped us through an even more substantial fix of the Jeep just moments earlier.

We both thought, "If we work harder, we can figure this out! How hard can this be?"

Well, God shut down our self-reliance and had us refocus on him. We should have asked God for help because he wants us to and apart from him we are nothing. "Ask and it will be given to you; seek and you will find; knock and the door will be opened to you. For everyone who asks receives; the one who seeks finds; and to the one who knocks, the door will be opened" (Matthew 7:7,8).

The prophet Hosea told the people to "wait for your God always" (Hosea 12:6). That word *always* is a big word, isn't it? Ben and I were praying to God and waiting on him when we were worried about how we would pay for a big repair on the Jeep, but God wants us to pray for the little things in life as well. He wants us waiting on him even when we think there's nothing to worry about. He isn't just the God who heals the sick or the God who helps us share the gospel with others. He is also the God who helps us pass our test, the God who gives us patience when dealing with a difficult patient or coworker, the God who helps us find what we need in the grocery store. He's not only the God who helps fix a Jeep that won't start, but he's also the God who helps us switch out a headlight. What if we had been praying about the headlight too? I suppose God could have changed it into the right kind of bulb if he wanted to. He also could have kept us from getting so frustrated and cold. He could have helped us realize sooner that I had bought the wrong bulb. (Or what if I had been asking for God's help to buy the right bulb in the first place?) In the end, he helped us finish both the repair job we entrusted to him and the one we didn't. Mostly, he helped us see how quick we were to stop waiting on him. I am thankful for the grace God wrapped around us on that cold winter night.

YOUR TURN

- Do you find yourself leaning on God more during the difficult tasks in life and forgetting about him when it's a task or trial you think you can handle on your own?

- How can you be reminded to lean on God more in both the valleys and the mountains?

Peter

Another example of how people often place their timing in their own hands came to me from a Bible study on Peter, a disciple of Jesus. Ben and I are a part of a monthly small group Bible study with three other couples. It started when a couple from our church with whom we were already friends asked if we would like to do such a Bible study with two other couples they had in mind. We take turns meeting at each couple's house, and whoever is hosting provides a snack and, more important, plans and leads the Bible study. The topic is the host's choice. It has been fun for me to meet with friends I already enjoy hanging out with, but it has also been encouraging to grow with them and support them on a deeper level.

One of our studies was on Peter and how he was so eager to support Jesus that he was willing to kill a soldier to defend his friend. John 18:10,11 tells us, "Then Simon Peter, who had a sword, drew it and struck the high priest's servant, cutting off his right ear. (The servant's name was Malchus.) Jesus commanded Peter, 'Put your sword away! Shall I not drink the cup the Father has given me?' " Jesus did not need Peter to step in. Jesus knew he was going to die, and he was willing to die on the cross even though he had done nothing wrong. It was the only way to save all people of all time from all their faults and shortcomings, because all are sinful. Peter wanted to take the situation into his own hands, but Jesus showed him trust in the Father's plan.

Jesus knew his Father's will. He knew it was his Father's will for him to be arrested, disowned, and crucified—the death sentence Jesus didn't deserve was going to pay for all the wickedness in the world so that all of it could be forgiven.

Jesus had told Peter that this was the plan again and again. But there in the dark olive grove with their figures lit by torchlight, Peter became worried and afraid and decided Jesus needed his help, so he acted on his impulse of what he felt was right. Maybe he was worried and afraid even before Judas' men got there. Who wouldn't be with the way Jesus had been talking and acting in the Garden of Gethsemane?

"Put your sword back in its place," Jesus said to him, "for all who draw the sword will die by the sword. Do you think I cannot call on my Father, and he will at once put at my disposal more than twelve legions of angels? But how then would the Scriptures be fulfilled that say it must happen in this way?" (Matthew 26:52-54)

In our small group Bible study, we read from Luke 22:51 that Jesus healed the man by touching his ear. Jesus was so gracious to Peter: rebuking him, telling him why things needed to be done this way, and then healing the man's ear. Peter was completely undeserving of Jesus' kindness and understanding, but God was patient with and loved Peter, just like he is patient with and loves us.

I know sometimes I have felt like Peter. I have felt like I was losing control or the people I love most were threatened, and I reacted. I have held that sword in my hand, ready to swing at the soldier no matter the cost. I have been irrational and responded without God's help, looking to my own strength instead of seeking the strength of the One who created me. Thank goodness for the grace God has shown me (and continues to show me), just like he showed Peter in the garden.

TRAVEL TIPS: Accountability Partners

It is important to find a dedicated accountability partner before beginning a 180 journey. Below are some pointers to keep in mind when deciding whom to ask:

♺ Choose someone who is going to be honest with you. You want someone who isn't afraid to ask if you are giving this project priority or why you haven't done your Bible study yet this week.

♺ Choose someone who is there for you—someone you can see in person, talk to on the phone, or video chat with often. Perhaps it is best to set a day, say every Wednesday, to discuss progress on the topic, including how your daily praying and journaling and weekly Bible study are going.

♺ Choose someone who wants to follow Jesus and can fully understand the why of your project.

♺ Most important, make sure your accountability partner *wants* to be a part of this journey because, after all, it is a six-month commitment. The best accountability partner is someone doing the same 180 journey with you! This is not necessary, but it is ideal because he or she can relate to what you are experiencing throughout the various stages of the journey.

↻ Whether you pick your sibling, friend, or spouse, it does not matter. What does matter is that your partner has the above qualities. A partner who possesses these qualities will help you stay focused on your topic and keep you committed and consistent.

↻ My accountability partner for this project was my husband, Ben. He has each one of these qualities. He isn't afraid to be honest with me and ask the tough questions. If he caught me worrying about something, he would often ask, "Have you been waiting on God more?" He saw me all the time at home, and that meant he saw me at my worst, when I wasn't motivated or I wanted to skip journaling just once because I was exhausted. He depends on Jesus for so much. He attends church with me, prays with me, goes to small group Bible study with me, and reads the Bible with me. He also inspired some ideas for the layout of the book and was a great sounding board for the various ideas I had on the topic. If I had to do it all over again, I would still pick Ben. I journaled about Ben and his accountability on day 25:

Today for some reason I was feeling worried and nervous about some things. Tonight when I was talking with Ben about these things, Ben goes, "I know, you should read a book called 'The 180 Series: Waiting On God More.'" And just like that he put it all in perspective.

↻ Are you feeling motivated to start the 180 journey but do not have someone in mind who fits the above qualities for an accountability partner? Pray. Pray that God places someone in your life (or brings forward someone you already know) who will be that sounding board and isn't afraid to ask those tough questions. You may have to wait on God a bit to bring forth that accountability partner.

House Hunting

Woah! Crazy day. We wrote an offer on a house we saw this morning. It's completely updated and move-in ready on a half of an acre lot. Talk about waiting. Ben and I prayed about it, and we were led to believe that we should buy this home. We met with Scott our realtor and signed the papers, and we'll know by Saturday noon if the offer has been accepted. More waiting and relying on God. Lord, help us keep focused on you, and to not get soaked up in worldly desires. Amen. [Day 21 of 180]

Waiting, waiting . . . and without me even thinking much about it this morning, we got the phone call from Scott [our realtor] around 10 A.M. My heart starts racing, Ben's voice on the phone was wavering. Were they going to accept, counter, or deny? It was all out of our hands. My mind kind of went numb, but then I started praying.

Our offer was accepted.

Ben and I were ecstatic! It was all sort of surreal to us. How could God be this good to us?! Actually, we were both very calm about this decision. It just felt "right." I think the reason it felt right was because we left this decision up to God. We've prayed about it and tried to not worry about it. [Day 23 of 180]

Maybe you can think of a time when you thought you knew what you wanted and had it all figured out, but then things changed and didn't bend your way. Maybe you realized later that the outcome was even greater than what you were thinking! This seems to happen to me often.

When Ben and I were hunting for our first home, we were pretty set that we wanted a fixer-upper on a property of three acres or more. Ben had worked for his dad's home remodeling business throughout high school and part of college. This experience provided him with handy fixer-upper skills. The first house we fell in love with fit exactly what we wanted: five acres of beautiful property with a mini orchard, including a variety of apple and pear trees, and a secluded wooded area. It even had a private field in the back that would be ideal for playing Ultimate Frisbee with our friends. It was perfect! The only problem was that it was the first house we had ever toured, and we felt it would be unwise to buy the first house we stepped foot into without looking at others. We also wanted to sound wise to our friends and family by saying that we had looked at other houses.

We booked four more houses to tour a couple of days later. About 20 minutes before we needed to leave for the showings, we checked the realtor's website, and the orchard house we had fallen in love with had just received and accepted an offer. We were so bummed! "How can any house compare?" we thought. Now that our orchard house was off the market, we went into these other home showings feeling bummed. We felt no house was ever going to be as perfect for us as the orchard house we fell in love with. The first three houses we toured that day were extremely disappointing. I knew after being in those homes for five minutes that they were not the right house we were looking for. The last house, however, we were pleasantly surprised by. Ironically, it was the house I had added to our showings at the last minute simply based on the location of the home, not necessarily the pictures of the home itself. Upon walking in, we were surprised by how different it looked from the photos online. It had been completely updated about two years prior with high-end upgrades like granite countertops in the kitchen and hardwood floors in the bedrooms. It was in a subdivision and on only half an acre, which was the minimum amount of land we wanted. It was as if whoever took the photos for the listing thought, "Let me find the worst angle possible to make the house look super small and leave all of the shades closed so it looks like it hasn't seen daylight in months." The photos did not exemplify the wonderful features of the home, which is probably why the house hadn't seen a lot of traffic.

A couple of things made the house not perfectly perfect. The previous owner was a smoker. We don't think the previous owner smoked inside the house because the smoke odor wasn't overpowering, but it was definitely present. Also the house seemed dark, like there weren't enough windows. It was packed full of the previous owner's heavy furniture, and none of the shades were open. The cramped and dark interior coupled with the smoke smell did not initially ring, "This is it!" However, we were able to look beyond the house's very minor imperfections and feel like they were fixable. We could repaint rooms to get rid of the smell and could purge the house of all the draperies, which harbor smoke. We could also have the carpet cleaned or even replaced. For extra measure, we could run an ozone machine to help eradicate the smell. We also knew that after the previous owner's furniture and draperies were moved out of the house, the house would feel much brighter and more spacious.

We thought and prayed about it and put an offer on the house the very next day. The market was hot at the time, so we felt we had to act fast! I think the poor-quality photos of the home and the smoke smell worked in our favor, as the house had received less traffic than other houses. We found out two days later that our offer was accepted. We were thrilled to move in to this move-in ready home. And it has really become home. The journal entry above was what I wrote down that day.

We quickly learned to love our little yard with no orchard. We bought a cute patio set for the concrete slab patio in our backyard and ate dinner outside any chance we could get. We also dug out a firepit. We were thankful that we didn't have to buy an expensive riding lawn mower. We had been renting a duplex, and as part of the contract we were required to care for the lawn. We often joked that it took more time to take the mower out of the garage than it did to mow the lawn. Now as first-time homeowners, half an acre seems like the perfect amount of land to manage without being overwhelmed. Sometimes I think about what it would have been like managing five acres with all the various fruit trees and vegetable gardens, and I'm thankful for managing a long and narrow plot of vegetables and a handful of annual flower beds.

This house is perfect for us first-time homebuyers. We didn't have to stress about Ben spending every ounce of his time making the house livable. We could just live right away in our house and not worry about renovations and living among dust and power tools. Another nice thing about our home is a full, unfinished basement with a walkout patio. This blank slate is perfect for Ben to scratch his remodeling and project itch and keep the project mess contained to one area. Our home is a ranch with three small bedrooms on the main floor and larger common spaces like the kitchen and living areas. There is plenty of space, so we do not feel like we need to rush the basement project. When we do end up finishing the basement, it will add a large amount of square footage and equity to our home.

In the end, God provided exactly what he wanted us to have. He didn't give us the first house we loved. Who knows the exact reasons why? Maybe that mini orchard would have been too much to handle. Maybe living in our remodeling mess would have been too stressful for us. Maybe the commute to Milwaukee for work would have become too long for me. Maybe working on that home or the home itself would have become an idol in our lives. We don't know the exact reasons, but we do know why we love our current house. We love that it's almost exactly in the center of our places of work. We love that it's only three minutes away from the freeway. We love the updates the home already had and the finishing touches we have added. We love that we are still only a 25- to 30-minute drive from Milwaukee.

Ben and I had been pretty bummed at losing the orchard house, as if our timing had been off. It felt like a huge missed opportunity. What I've learned, though, is God's timing is perfect. I don't even think about our first love, the orchard house. I am content where we are and thankful for God's timing.

It's interesting to me to look back and see how God works and how great his timing is. It was a blessing that I was actively on my 180 journey of waiting on God more during this time in my life. Buying a house is supposed to be a stressful thing, but because my focus was shifted to relying on God, buying a house felt easy. I joked that it was way easier than buying a car, even though the ticket price was ten times more! Ben and I are grateful. Buying a house and having the option to choose one and its amenities is something not many people get to experience. We are humbled by how much God has blessed us.

If I hadn't been concentrating on waiting on God more, I think I would have had a different perspective. I would have been a lot more upset if I hadn't been reminding myself of Jesus and his promises and praying to him. God was gracious, and he taught Ben and me that what seemed to be bad luck, a closed door, or poor timing was in reality his way of having us rely on him completely. We were able to watch his promises come true. He blessed us beyond what we could imagine!

YOUR TURN

- Have you ever experienced a time when you thought you knew what was best for you, but then God proved you wrong and gave you something even better?

- Have you ever experienced a time when you anxiously waited for God to say yes to your request, but he didn't give you what you wanted? What do you think he was teaching you during this time?

Politics

Today is election day. Everyone is posting selfies of "I voted" stickers. I'm proud to be an American in this democracy. However, not many are proud of the candidates that are running. It's a good reminder for me that our citizenship is not bound to this earth. Our inheritance in fact is in heaven. [Day 111 of 180]

So much talk after the election today. I have two main thoughts. 1) God uses the unlikely for his kingdom. 2) The devil is thriving on all of this backlash post-election. [Day 112 of 180]

It can be easy as Christians to forget that God is in control of our nation. I feel like this is especially true around election time. A change in earthly power often brings about many questions of what the future will hold. This causes anxiety and chaos. The nominees in presidential elections, or any elections, have their flaws. There are often horrible accusations against each of them, which makes choosing one incredibly difficult. I'm not going to get political in a Democrat versus Republican sort of way. But what I observed from the pre-election hoopla during my 180 was that all the waiting and uncertainty that goes on brings about the worst in people: waiting for the results of the primary, waiting for the debates, waiting for election day, waiting for the results of election day.

On every election day, approximately 50 percent of people in the United States are disappointed with the results because their candidate lost. People take to social media platforms to state their opinions, and it becomes toxic in many cases. There are unhealthy discussions and misplaced accusations. There are awful memes and straight up untrue news articles written about the candidates. What the election taught me was how much I hold dear the fact that heaven is my true home. There are fallible leaders because all are sinful, but I do know that God can and does work even through the worst of leaders. I do know that Jesus is King.

On the other hand, the devil is powerful, and he uses the negativity to his advantage to create doubt and fear. The devil causes people to put their trust in their earthly leaders to fix their problems instead of placing their trust in God.

C. S. Lewis' book *The Screwtape Letters* is about an experienced demon, Screwtape, giving advice to an amateur demon, Wormwood, on his "patient"—a new Christian he is trying to lead astray. It gives us a small glimpse into the devil's deceptive and intelligent mind. During the lead-up to the election while I was journaling, a quote attributed to this book was circulating on social media. The quote is a clever fake, but it is interesting. Even though C. S. Lewis didn't write it, it has a vivid and worthwhile point to make. It shows how politics can give us a warped perspective.

My dear Wormwood,

Be sure that the patient remains completely fixated on politics. Arguments, political gossip, and obsessing on the faults of people they have never met serves as an excellent distraction from advancing in personal virtue, character, and the things the patient can control. Make sure to keep the patient in a constant state of angst, frustration, and general disdain towards the rest of the human race in order to avoid any kind of charity or inner peace from further developing. Ensure the patient continues to believe that the problem is "out there" in the "broken system" rather than recognizing there is a problem with himself.

Keep up the good work,

Uncle Screwtape

Surrounding the election, it seemed like there was hate, violence, hysteria, and rioting everywhere. What does this solve? Nothing. It's just the devil pulling us away from the issues at hand, like our eternal well-being. He enjoys seeing polarizing opinions in politics within our families. He feeds on the lies and backhanded comments. Focusing all our attention on the polls takes away from time spent in prayer and reading our Bibles.

During the election, I had to learn again that though the devil is powerful, God is even more powerful. God is ultimately in control over any president. I'll continue to wait on God to show me his unwavering power because I know for a fact that the president, any president, will let me down. But God won't! This is yet another example where I feel like God is setting up a clear picture of our need for a Savior. The search for fulfillment from a political leader will only leave me feeling empty, lied to, and let down. What I do know is this: Jesus fulfills every aspect of my life in which every political leader fails. This truth I cling to day after day!

Joseph

God has many examples of waiting in the Bible, probably because it's a part of the way God draws us closer to him. A great example of waiting during political strife, as well as during family problems, is Joseph. Joseph was a son of Jacob and was his father's favorite son. Jacob even gave him a coat of many colors. Joseph's brothers were jealous, and they grew even more jealous when Joseph shared that he had dreams of his brothers bowing down to him, represented by 11 stars bowing to Joseph. The brothers had had enough of their seemingly perfect brother, and they took the opportunity that presented itself to sell Joseph into slavery in Egypt when he was a teenager. During Joseph's time in Egypt, he went from being a slave to being the head of Potiphar's household (Potiphar was one of Pharoah's officials) to being thrown into prison (he was wrongly accused by Potiphar's wife of sexually assaulting her) to being second-in-command to Pharaoh over the land of Egypt. Even when Joseph was in prison under false accusations, God still was there with him, guiding and blessing him. God gave him the ability to interpret two prisoners' dreams, and they both came true. Pharaoh heard of this and asked if Joseph could interpret his dreams. This job of dream interpretation was what landed Joseph into Pharoah's favor and out of prison.

God ultimately blessed Joseph. He became one of the richest men in Egypt, he was respected by many, he saved Egypt and the surrounding areas from a severe famine for seven years, and he was able to see his father and brothers once again and to forgive them. All of this did not happen overnight. No, it took years, and it was over a decade before he saw his family again face-to-face. So much waiting. I feel like if I were Joseph, I would become impatient and I would probably hold a grudge against my siblings. Joseph didn't do this because God was working on his heart for years, and Joseph understood contentment in rough situations.

Joseph is an amazing example of contentment. The apostle Paul also speaks of contentment. He says:

> I am not saying this because I am in need, for I have
> learned to be content whatever the circumstances. I know
> what it is to be in need, and I know what it is to have

plenty. I have learned the secret of being content in any and every situation, whether well fed or hungry, whether living in plenty or in want. I can do all this through him who gives me strength. (Philippians 4:11-13)

Joseph had plenty of time to hold grudges; he even had the power to get even with his brothers who sold him into slavery. But we don't hear of this from Joseph. And we don't hear of Paul complaining about his circumstances or see a lack of motivation from him to continue sharing the gospel. Both of these heroes of faith endured imprisonment and much waiting, but we see how they relied on God and shifted their focus and energy to ways they could serve and honor God instead of wallowing in their trials.

Amy

The first time I met Amy was a cold, snowy day in February. Ben and his family have a long-standing tradition of over 30 years: Every February, they travel to the Northwoods near Hayward, Wisconsin, about an hour drive from Lake Superior. This long weekend getaway includes relaxation, good food, company, and a lot of cross-country skiing. Ben and his dad, along with other family members, participate in the American Birkebeiner, a 55-kilometer cross-country ski race through gorgeous Wisconsin woods. This race is the largest in North America, drawing 13,000 participants each year from all over the world. Skiing is a sport that Ben's family lives and breathes, and Ben and his siblings were all taught to ski as soon as they could walk.

So there we all were, over 20 of us, packed into a rental cabin, filled with excitement over what the next days would bring, and there was a new face in the room. I remember Amy's striking, gorgeous dark brown eyes and smooth light brown skin. She was one year old at the time she was introduced to our family and had been put into foster care and placed in the home of family members a few weeks prior to our trip. The ultimate goal of fostering was adoption.

It had all started one year earlier. Talking about adoption was not new; our family members, a married couple, had talked about it on and off since they were dating as something they'd maybe do someday. But it was not something either of them was focusing on at that point in their life. Right then, their focus was on raising their two-and-a-half-year-old son and four-month-old daughter. The couple both happened to listen—separately but on the same day—to the same podcast episode about adoption and letting God write your family's story: The wife was listening at home while doing the dishes, and the husband was listening at work. For both of them, the podcast ignited a sudden sense of urgency to adopt. How crazy it was that they had listened to the same podcast and had felt the same strong push to start looking into adoption immediately. Their life seemed comfortable with their perfect little family in their new house. It was almost shocking to them that they felt such a strong push to pursue something so life-altering when life was so enjoyable and predictable.

Soon after listening to the podcast, the couple began to explore international adoption. They felt it would be less messy than fostering with their young family. They attended an international adoption meeting, but they left feeling that it was not where God wanted them to be at the time.

Our relatives thought the door for adoption had closed, and they returned to their normal lives. Little did they know what God had in store. They started seeing signs for fostering everywhere it seemed: billboards on the highway, news stories, and conversations with friends. They slowly felt their hearts soften to the idea of fostering even though they knew it was a messy process. If their reasons for wanting to pursue adoption were based on godly motivations, didn't those same reasons apply to fostering? They decided to prayerfully take a step, thinking, "If God doesn't want us to go down the foster care route, he can definitely stop us. But we will always feel that we told God no if we aren't even willing to look into it."

The couple decided to attend a foster care informational meeting, and again they felt overwhelmed, intimidated, and not sure what they should do. They prayed that if God wanted them to take another step, he would make that very clear.

Later that same day, the couple attended a family friend's graduation party. At that party, the first people they were introduced to were an older Christian couple with a little baby girl they had been fostering. This little girl was Amy. At the party, this kind couple, who had been emergency fostering for many years, encouraged our relatives not to get overwhelmed by the process but to continue to pursue fostering. The reminder was that these kids were worth fighting for and it was important for Christians to step up and bring them into homes that would share the truth of Jesus.

Encouraged by this conversation with these new friends and feeling God's hand once again pushing them forward, our relatives stepped out in faith and began the foster care licensing process. It took over six months to complete the home study, take classes, and become a licensed foster home by the state they lived in.

The couple had always imagined they would be fostering a boy, but over the course of a week, two separate people stopped by their home with bins of girl clothes for their daughter who was almost one year old. It was enough clothes to share with another little girl the same age.

Then they received an email from the couple they had met at the graduation party, asking them if they would be interested in fostering to potentially adopt the little girl they had with them at the party. They were shocked and excited. God was clearly guiding their steps, and they continued to prayerfully keep moving forward. It wasn't as simple as just saying yes. While waiting for the licensing process to finish, they babysat the little girl multiple times and became a respite provider for her. Months later, the state decided to place the child in their home. So there Amy was, immersed in this new Christ-centered family with a sister four months older and a brother three years older.

Like many kids in the foster care system, Amy experienced emotional trauma that often displayed itself in an unhealthy anxiety over food. Kids from hard situations will often look to food as a coping mechanism for comfort and security. In Amy's case, her food anxieties were very strong and challenging to manage. It wasn't uncommon for her to eat until she was sick, steal food, or scream uncontrollably at the end of meals. She also struggled with attachment, especially with her foster mom, and that was challenging and emotional to navigate. But slowly over time, these problems lessened as the Holy Spirit worked hard to calm Amy's heart. When studying psychology, you learn that the environment has a lot to do with a person's development. In a steady Christian home with a whole family to love her, Amy was in a wonderful place to heal and grow. Unconditional love from her parents and love and friendship from her siblings were a huge blessing for her. However, I think it was more than just her environment that shaped and changed her. I think it was the Holy Spirit working on her through his Word and her new family, helping her overcome her insecurities and find love in Christ and joy in her salvation even at such a young age.

In the months and years since I first met Amy at the skiing cabin, I have watched the little miracles happen. I watched her leave her dinner unfinished one night so she could go play with the other kids. I watched her initiate play with her cousins willingly instead of being told by her parents to play. At first, new places and vacations made her nervous, but then our family spent a week in Tennessee, and she said she never wanted to leave there. At our most recent annual Northwoods adventure, she proved us wrong again. The rest of her family got a stomach flu and had to leave early, and Amy just sobbed and sobbed, not wanting to go. I normally wouldn't say it was good to see a child cry because she had to leave early from a vacation, but in this case it was so good to see Amy cry. Those tears meant she had bonded with her family, even her extended family. Those tears meant she was beginning to make memories on vacation. Those tears meant she was loved and she belonged. When she responded "normally" to these situations, we celebrated because of what it meant for the healing of her wounded heart.

It took four years for Amy to be officially adopted. The courts were messy. Schedules and appointments kept getting delayed and delayed. Both of her biological parents appealed when the courts determined that termination of parental rights was in her best interest.

Court date delays were among the hardest parts of the journey. Nothing our relatives could say or do would schedule them sooner. This helplessness was the hardest part for this foster mother. She learned through all these trials that she liked to be in control and have a chance to fix things. With Amy's emotional challenges and attachment struggles, and most certainly with the drawn-out court case, God was continually teaching her new parents to step back and let him take control. They learned to wait on God.

Other times they wanted to take things into their own hands were when they had to send Amy alone on visits with one of her biological parents. It was especially challenging because they could see how difficult it was for Amy to process and emotionally handle these situations at such a young age. It took her days to settle back down after these visits. They wanted to just fix it all somehow. They were so frustrated and felt like they had no voice.

Then, for a while, everything pointed to the full restoration of parental rights to one of Amy's biological parents. Knowing the history of the case, our relatives knew that it would have been a bad situation, but they were powerless to do anything. They had to trust that God had a plan and pray for him to fight for their little girl when they could not. And he did! Just when the court seemed on the brink of reunifying Amy with one of her parents, God allowed the courts to see the truth and all visits were stopped and never started again.

Amy was officially adopted. The judge was joyful, and it was a wonderful day! The family celebrated at a restaurant that day, and a few weeks later they threw a large adoption party at their church's gym, complete with great food and a bounce obstacle course. You could tell Amy was having the time of her life! She called herself "Adoption Girl" for months afterward, and she played adoption with her now-official siblings. Her excitement and joy over her adoption is a great reminder, to me personally, of how excited we should be over our adoption into Christ's family—so excited that joy just pours out of us. One day during the most challenging transition after Amy moved into their home, her adoptive mom was reflecting on how the family had gotten into this crazy journey, and she became curious about what day she had listened to the adoption podcast. It was on that cold winter day that God had obviously used the podcast to get both parents thinking about adoption. When she looked up the specific episode of the podcast, she saw that it had aired on the exact day of Amy's birth! My husband doesn't care for the phrase "it's a God thing" because he feels like it's used so much that it's lost its meaning—even used by non-Christians who don't believe God's hand does anything in anyone's life. But this really, truly is worthy of the status "God thing." God has a plan for Amy's life, and while it includes the brokenness of her early life, it also includes his beautiful plan of redemption. Amy was always meant to be part of her adoptive family. Psalm 139:16 says, "Your eyes saw my unformed body; all the days ordained for me were written in your book before one of them came to be." God knows the twists and turns of our lives, and he knew that even though Amy was born into a messy situation, he would place her adoptive family members into her life to love her and call her their own. It was inspiring for me to watch the journey of Amy's adoption. Was the journey easy? No way. It was a hard adjustment for the family, and it involved many sacrifices, hard lessons, humbling situations, and parenting mistakes. But the blessings they've seen have been worth it. God wasn't just working in Amy's life; he was softening and changing the hearts of her new parents as well. He was teaching them grace, perseverance, and trust in his plan. It's easy to think what a great fit their family was for Amy and how much she has been influenced by their loving and caring Christlike attitude, but I think sometimes the extended family members forget how much Amy has taught all of them. She has taught them patience, unwavering love, and not to underestimate what she is capable of.

Our family came to understand more fully that God's timing is not our timing and that he sees things from a long-term perspective, whereas we become caught up in the day-to-day waiting. The adoption process was hung up in the messy court system for four years. Four years of no finalization, four years of the unknown, four years of delayed court dates, and four years of constant adjustment as a family structure. It was also four years of living and breathing waiting on God. Prayer became essential, and as God worked in the mess, our relatives slowly began to find more peace in the process. They feel like in the four years of fostering Amy they have grown in ways that they would have never done if God hadn't taken them where he did.

Where did these amazing parents get their strength and energy from? Where did they get the strength to drop Amy off at visits when they knew they were hard for her? Where did they find solace and peace when it felt like nothing was going right? It was through Christ.

> We do not lose heart. Though outwardly we are wasting away, yet inwardly we are being renewed day by day. For our light and momentary troubles are achieving for us an eternal glory that far outweighs them all. So we fix our eyes not on what is seen, but on what is unseen, since what is seen is temporary, but what is unseen is eternal.
> (2 Corinthians 4:16-18)

God reminds us that our "momentary troubles" are nothing compared to our "eternal glory that far outweighs them all." Throughout our challenging times, God's Word keeps our focus on what is unseen: the promise of eternal life in heaven. This makes our loads a little bit lighter, remembering that troubles in this life come and go, but God's grace is steadfast. God's Word reminds us:

Since we have been justified through faith, we have peace with God through our Lord Jesus Christ, through whom we have gained access by faith into this grace in which we now stand. And we boast in the hope of the glory of God. Not only so, but we also glory in our sufferings, because we know that suffering produces perseverance; perseverance, character; and character, hope. And hope does not put us to shame, because God's love has been poured out into our hearts through the Holy Spirit, who has been given to us. (Romans 5:1-5)

Looking retrospectively, Amy's parents can see clearly how God guided them through the process, even during those times that felt impossible to conquer. They were also encouraged by the fact that they had to surrender to God and focus completely on the race he set before them.

YOUR TURN

- Has there been a time in your life when you have felt hopeless? Maybe something legally is out of your control?

- Whom or what did you rely on when you were waiting in the trenches?

- How can you encourage others who are struggling as they wait for something in their life to finalize or have closure?

Could You Adopt?

Observing Amy's parents maneuver through the ups and downs of their journey has been truly inspiring to me and others around them. When I tell people this story, the most common responses are things like, "Wow, she must have a lot of patience! That's just not for me. Too messy." And they're right. There are so many unknowns with a foster or adoption situation: What kind of child will be placed in my home? Will the child have special needs? What if the child has visits with his or her biological parents? What if my own biological children become attached to the foster child, and then the foster child is pulled to a different home? What if the child has attachment issues with me?

If I only concentrated on the above questions, I would worry myself sick and talk myself out of fostering as fast as I talked myself into it. But if you think about the child, the perspective changes. Think about a child in need who's in a rough spot, and if you knew the child and his or her story, face, and name, wouldn't it be hard to refuse to take this child into your home? Foster care isn't glamorous, but it's an act that, if done with godly motives, is completely selfless.

In fact, God calls us, his children, to take care of those in need, especially orphans. Notice how this Bible passage mentions the fatherless: "Defend the weak and the fatherless; uphold the cause of the poor and the oppressed. Rescue the weak and the needy; deliver them from the hand of the wicked" (Psalm 82:3,4). God also tells us that if we welcome a child in need *in Jesus' name,* we are welcoming God into our homes. "Whoever welcomes one of these little children in my name welcomes me; and whoever welcomes me does not welcome me but the one who sent me" (Mark 9:37). Welcoming a child in Jesus' name means we welcome that child because we love Jesus. We naturally desire to serve others with God's love because God loved us first and sent Jesus to save us. God reminds us not only to welcome and love others but also to stand up for those who are unable to stand up for themselves. In Amy's case, she wasn't an orphan per se, but her biological parents were not fit to parent her. She needed someone to speak up for her, especially in the courtroom. "Speak up for those who cannot speak for themselves, for the rights of all who are destitute. Speak up and judge fairly; defend the rights of the poor and needy" (Proverbs 31:8,9).

As of right now, I am unsure if Ben and I would ever adopt or foster. I guess you could say I'm waiting on God. I'm not trying to guilt anyone reading this book into adopting or fostering. Rather, what I want to share with everyone is how I was encouraged to see how waiting on God for four years has blessed these parents' relationships with Christ, each other, their biological children, and Amy. On the other hand, God has given us all gifts and talents to use and further his kingdom. If you have what it takes to welcome into your home a child who needs it, I pray that you will ask God to give you strength and wisdom to do so. The journey is not always rainbows and butterflies, but that's because we're sinful and broken people in need of a Savior.

Did You Know?

When you think about it, we are all adopted. We are all adopted children of God. Jesus sacrificed his life on the cross for us so that we are welcomed into his family and have a spot in heaven. Because we are adopted, we can be confident of our life after earth. We understand who holds the world in his hands, and this gives us great confidence in this life as well as in the next.

It took Amy a long time to lower her defenses and allow her new parents to love her. Initially she seemed to push away their love. As stubborn human beings, this is how we respond to God's love at times. We know that God loves us and would do anything for us, but instead of humbly admitting that we don't deserve God's love, we *act* like we think God might not deserve *our* love. We lie, we put our wants and desires first, we gossip and ruin someone's good name, and the list goes on. Any time we sin, it's like we're saying to God, "I don't care if you say you're my dad: I don't have to listen to you." How that hurts him! We are completely undeserving of his love, yet he has adopted us. "See what great love the Father has lavished on us, that we should be called children of God! And that is what we are! The reason the world does not know us is that it did not know him" (1 John 3:1). Adoptive parents can understand on a new level how much God loves us. Every day Amy's family sees her, they feel a small part of how it must feel for God our Father when he looks at us his children. As a believer, I wait for the day when my body is glorified and I can be with God face-to-face. I think it will be the same kind of rejoicing as there was at Amy's official adoption. The Bible says, "We ourselves, who have the firstfruits of the Spirit, groan inwardly as we wait eagerly for our adoption to sonship, the redemption of our bodies" (Romans 8:23). Eagerly waiting is easier when we consider the joy that is to come.

TRAVEL TIPS: Discovery

What I've discovered on this 180 journey is that God is full of surprises. It's one thing to know God's beautiful and unwavering grace, but it's another thing to completely rely on his grace and see it in everyday life. Throughout my journey, I had time to reflect on previous experiences. Much of Amy's story happened before my 180 journey, but after reflecting on her journey to adoption, I realized how much waiting her family had to endure on so many different levels. God brought the story to the forefront of my mind, and I discovered a lot about waiting. That made me think of some encouragements for you readers.

↻ I encourage you, during your 180, to remember moments like I did. Consider past experiences that just clicked with you. Reflect on and try to understand the gravity of those moments.

↻ As you are immersed in a subject, like waiting on God more, take some time to pray that God brings forth past experiences for you to glean from during your journey.

Faith Hall of Fame

Have you ever read the faith hall of fame (as some call it) in Hebrews chapter 11? It's worth a closer look, whether you are reading it for the first time or have read it many times before. What a great testament it is to what faith can do. While I was writing this book, my small group Bible study dove into this chapter. Three people in this hall of fame especially stuck with me as those who exemplified waiting on God. Abraham is highlighted in Hebrews chapter 11:

> By faith Abraham, when God tested him, offered Isaac as a sacrifice. He who had embraced the promises was about to sacrifice his one and only son, even though God had said to him, "It is through Isaac that your offspring will be reckoned." Abraham reasoned that God could even raise the dead, and so in a manner of speaking he did receive Isaac back from death. (Hebrews 11:17-19)

For Abraham, the willingness to sacrifice his son was an act of faith. I can't even imagine what thoughts were racing through his mind. Abraham knew the line of Christ would come through his son, Isaac, so he put his trust in God's promises. It seems crazy to us that Abraham trusted God so much that he was willing to kill his son. He was willing to break the ethical and moral rules of his people. He was willing to be disowned by his family and friends for this act. He was willing to sacrifice his reputation, friends, and family due to his belief in God and his divine will. How hard it must have been for Abraham to travel with his son for three days, all the time waiting to see how God was going to undo this terrifying and gruesome command. So much waiting and, I'd imagine, a lot of silence and time to think, reflect, and pray. The Bible does not say what Abraham was thinking during these three long days, but I know if I were Abraham, I would probably be having an internal war about whether or not to go through with this command. I would be thinking of the aftermath of such an act and how it would affect *me*. But Abraham did not place limits on God. He knew that God can even raise the dead. Abraham followed God's command and even went as far as binding Isaac on top of the altar and having the knife in hand about to slay his son before God stopped him moments before he would have taken his son's life. And then God provided a different sacrifice for the altar (Genesis 22:9-13).

Moses is another person highlighted as one of great faith in this section of Hebrews, even giving up a comfortable life. "He chose to be mistreated along with the people of God rather than to enjoy the fleeting pleasures of sin" (Hebrews 11:25). Moses was the leader of God's people through the Red Sea, across the desert, and up to the Promised Land. He also had to endure much waiting. After leaving Egypt in confusion and fear, he had to wait 40 years before God spoke to him in the burning bush (Exodus chapters 2,3). He had to wait through ten plagues before Pharaoh finally gave in and let the Israelites go. He had to wander in the wilderness for 40 years because the Israelites didn't trust God, and then he didn't even get to go into the Promised Land. It was a lot of waiting!

Moses was a great leader, but his greatness didn't come from something within him; it came from stepping out in faith. When God asked Moses to lead the Israelites out of Egypt, Moses questioned God, "Who am I that I should go to Pharaoh and bring the Israelites out of Egypt?" (Exodus 3:11). After God reassured Moses that he would be with him, Moses questioned God some more, "Suppose I go to the Israelites and say to them, 'The God of your fathers has sent me to you,' and they ask me, 'What is his name?' Then what shall I tell them?" (Exodus 3:13). God simply told him what to say, "I AM has sent me to you" (Exodus 3:14).

Moses once again questioned God, "What if they do not believe me or listen to me and say, 'The LORD did not appear to you'?" (Exodus 4:1). God then proceeded to give Moses three miraculous signs to prove he was sent by the Lord: (1) when Moses threw his staff on the ground, the staff would become a snake; (2) when he placed his hand inside his cloak and pulled it back out, his hand would be leprous; and (3) when he took water from the Nile River and poured it on the ground, the water would turn into blood. Even after these three miraculous signs, Moses still doubted. "Pardon your servant, Lord. I have never been eloquent, neither in the past nor since you have spoken to your servant. I am slow of speech and tongue" (Exodus 4:10). To this God replied, "Who gave human beings their mouths? Who makes them deaf or mute? Who gives them sight or makes them blind? Is it not I, the LORD? Now go; I will help you speak and will teach you what to say" (Exodus 4:11,12).

Moses once more pled to the Lord, "Pardon your servant, Lord. Please send someone else" (Exodus 4:13). God was gracious to Moses, although we see in Exodus 4:14 that "the LORD's anger burned against Moses." God promised that he would give Moses the words to speak and would also provide help from Moses' brother, Aaron, who spoke well. Talk about God being patient with Moses! It seemed like Moses had every excuse in the book *not* to do what God had asked him to do. But God still used Moses and blessed him greatly despite his qualms, hesitation, and disbelief early on. Honestly, I think I'd be the same way. I think what makes the story of Moses so special is that he didn't do everything as perfectly as he could have. He didn't just say, "Yes, Lord," at God's first request. He continued to question God repeatedly. Yet God uses imperfect people to fulfill his will. If God could use Moses, he can use imperfect me as well.

One person who surprised me to be noted in the faith hall of fame section is Rahab. Joshua, the leader of the Israelites after Moses, sent two spies into the city of Jericho in Canaan to investigate because Canaan was God's Promised Land for the Israelites. Rahab was a prostitute who lived in Jericho, and she hid the Israelite spies in her home. Because Rahab made good on her promise not to tell the king of Jericho that the Israelites were still in her home, hiding under stalks of flax on her roof, God spared her and her family during the battle in Jericho. She demonstrated her faith in her words to the spies:

> I know that the LORD has given you this land and that a great fear of you has fallen on us, so that all who live in this country are melting in fear because of you. We have heard how the LORD dried up the water of the Red Sea for you when you came out of Egypt, and what you did to Sihon and Og, the two kings of the Amorites east of the Jordan, whom you completely destroyed. When we heard of it, our hearts melted in fear and everyone's courage failed because of you, for the LORD your God is God in heaven above and on the earth below. (Joshua 2:9-11)

As soon as the people asking about the spies left, Rahab told the spies to hide in the hills for three days. She acted quickly and decisively to save the Israelite spies and went out of her way to hide them. In doing so, she made the declaration, "The LORD your God is God in heaven above and on the earth below." It was a simple declaration of faith, but it was so powerful!

Before sending the spies off to hide, Rahab pleaded with them, "Now then, please swear to me by the LORD that you will show kindness to my family, because I have shown kindness to you" (Joshua 2:12).

The spies agreed. They told Rahab to tie a scarlet cord through her window and have her family in her home with her. They warned, "If any of them go outside your house into the street, their blood will be on their own heads; we will not be responsible. As for those who are in the house with you, their blood will be on our head if a hand is laid on them. But if you tell what we are doing, we will be released from the oath you made us swear" (Joshua 2:19,20). James tells us how important Rahab's faith was: "In the same way, was not even Rahab the prostitute considered righteous for what she did when she gave lodging to the spies and sent them off in a different direction?" (James 2:25).

I can picture Rahab looking out her front window, huddling together with her family, and watching the walls crumble down and the people being trapped under the rubble. If I were Rahab, I'm sure I would have doubted, wondering if the spies I had known only for a few days would keep their promise of saving my family and me. My instinct would probably be to run and try to escape the entire disaster, but Rahab did not run. She trusted. The spies had promised her safety. She had to wait. She waited to see if she would be saved. She waited to see if God would be gracious to her family and her and spare their lives. Her waiting was not in vain; God did save her.

During my 180, I've clung to various stories of the Bible to give me courage and inspire me to wait on God. Abraham, Moses, and Rahab all demonstrated trust in God and his timing. Abraham spent three days waiting on God as he traveled to sacrifice his son. Moses waited decades as the leader of the Israelites to enter the Promised Land. Rahab waited patiently in her home with her family, waiting on God to rescue her.

Dear Lord, help me be more trusting of you and your timing like these men and this woman of great faith were. Amen.

TRAVEL TIPS: Journaling

I've never been one to journal. In grade school and high school, I had a couple of close friends who journaled daily. I always admired them for doing so because I thought it would be neat to look back on what your high school self was thinking at that time. It may even be laughable to read what you felt insecure about back then (I think it was boys for me). I remember attempting to journal a couple of times in high school, but it would only ever last a few weeks. Journaling for 180 days (six months!) was much longer than I had ever done. I'm going to be honest—at first it felt like a chore, but somewhere in the middle I grew to enjoy it. Journaling is an important aspect of the 180 journey. Here are some journaling ideas for you.

♡ Deciding what to journal about is important. I journaled about the people in my life I observed to be waiting on God, the various things I was waiting on God for (or failing to wait on God for), and my studies in the Bible of what waiting on God really means. It's been enjoyable to look back on my journal entries and see how far I've come in learning to wait on God more.

♡ How and when to journal are also an important part of the journaling equation. For me, it was best to journal at night before bed, reflecting on the day's events. I am not a morning person, so waking up even earlier to journal before work sounded like a chore to me. However, the perfect time for you to reflect might be before your children are awake for the day or before you feel bogged down by the day's happenings.

♡ As far as the method of journaling, old-fashioned pen and paper work great, but an electronic method may be easier and faster for some. Pick whatever is best for you!

♡ I would say that consistency is key. If you choose to journal at night right after dinner, journal every night after dinner. People thrive on consistency and habit. The key is to make it a priority of everyday life, just like brushing your teeth before bed every night. Of course, if you know that you will be busy during your journaling time, pick a different time that day. It's most beneficial for you and this journey to journal every day!

A Time for Everything

Through my 180, I learned to take comfort in the fact that, as Christians, we can trust in God's timing. We can trust that he has a divine plan for us. I love this section from Ecclesiastes and take great comfort in its truth.

> There is a time for everything,
>> and a season for every activity under the heavens:
>> a time to be born and a time to die,
>> a time to plant and a time to uproot,
>> a time to kill and a time to heal,
>> a time to tear down and a time to build,
>> a time to weep and a time to laugh,
>> a time to mourn and a time to dance,
>> a time to scatter stones and a time to gather them,
>> a time to embrace and a time to refrain
>>> from embracing,
>> a time to search and a time to give up,
>> a time to keep and a time to throw away,
>> a time to tear and a time to mend,
>> a time to be silent and a time to speak,
>> a time to love and a time to hate,
>> a time for war and a time for peace.
>
> What do workers gain from their toil? I have seen the burden God has laid on the human race. He has made everything beautiful in its time. He has also set eternity in the human heart; yet no one can fathom what God has done from beginning to end. (Ecclesiastes 3:1-11)

The book of Ecclesiastes does not promise that God will let people know when the times are. When is the time to be silent? When is the time to speak? When can even hatred and war be transformed into something beautiful? Solomon's answer seems like it might be something "no one can fathom."

This section seems like an encouragement to wait on God, doesn't it? When will the time come for God to show the beauty in a particular situation in life? He doesn't say. That is part of the "burden God has laid on the human race." But he knows the beautiful time for *everything*. Wait for him.

Waiting on God Means Praying and Waiting for His Answers

Prayer = Communication

God's the one who "gets stuff done" in our life, but we claim that we "don't have enough time to pray to Him." Does that really make sense? [Day 47 of 180]

Journaling for six months straight about the things that try my patience led me to realize how often it frustrates me (okay, a *lot* of times) that doctors don't communicate with nurses. This was a common occurrence throughout my journal, especially when I wrote after a day at work. Yes, most doctors do communicate with nurses, but that is not always the case. It does not make sense why many doctors fail to communicate with nurses either in person or on the phone. It's important for doctors to let the nurses know the plan of care for the patient—to let us know if there's anything specific we should be assessing for or if there's an upcoming test or procedure. Often doctors place an order in the computer for an important task to be done, but we don't always know the rationale for the order, so we end up calling the provider for an explanation. In addition, we don't always see the order in a timely fashion because we are often busy caring for other patients and are not sitting at the computer constantly refreshing the orders tab. This gap in communication is frustrating for me as a bedside nurse who would like to know and understand the full plan so that I can educate my patients and better care for them. In a perfect world, nurses and doctors would become more of a team and have a multidisciplinary approach.

I may be biased, but I strongly believe that nurses are the glue of the hospital. Nurses actually do the work. They make sure the patient is cared for. They advocate for their patients. They administer all of their patients' daily medications, constantly assess patients for any slight change in condition, and provide appropriate interventions. They perform many important medical procedures. They orchestrate the dozens of appointments that patients have so none are missed. If a doctor puts in an order for a test, the nurses call the appropriate discipline and set up an appointment time. They make sure any dietary or activity restrictions are enforced and all orders that doctors place in the computer make sense and are correct. When patients are discharged, nurses provide education about the patients' conditions, send wound supplies home with them, and ensure they have a ride home. To sum it all up, nurses wear a ton of different hats: they are their patients' appointment keeper, cheerleader, confidant, transporter, and server.

All in all, nurses are the driving force of ensuring tasks are done timely and correctly, all while advocating for their patients. Nurses are the ones who get stuff done. They have many tasks on their plates, and having doctors fail to directly communicate with them is frustrating. As a health-care team, a hospital preaches that it is one team made up of various disciplines all working toward the goals of the patient. This is true, but at times it feels like each discipline is concentrating on its own tasks without taking into consideration the other disciplines. Sometimes the health-care team is so focused on its tasks that it neglects to listen to the patient's needs and wants.

As I reflected on my 180 journaling, I realized that as Christ's dearly beloved daughter, I do not practice perfect communication with God. In fact, I would say I fail miserably at it. After all, God is the only one who gets stuff done in life, similar to how nurses—on a much smaller scale and less significantly—get stuff done in the hospital. I say I don't have enough time to go to God. Does that make any sense? No, but I fail to go to him anyway. I say I don't know what to pray for. Yet God says, "In the same way, the Spirit helps us in our weakness. We do not know what we ought to pray for, but the Spirit himself intercedes for us through wordless groans" (Romans 8:26). God is so gracious to his children that even when we are suffering and do not have the words to speak, the Holy Spirit intercedes on our behalf! I need to learn to communicate with the God who gets stuff done.

So I pray. I pray that prayer becomes central and a priority in my life. God shows me his grace time and time again when I don't communicate with him. God wants his children to pray about anything and anyone, and there are no specific criteria.

> Is anyone among you in trouble? Let them pray. Is anyone happy? Let them sing songs of praise. Is anyone among you sick? Let them call the elders of the church to pray over them and anoint them with oil in the name of the Lord. And the prayer offered in faith will make the sick person well; the Lord will raise them up. If they have sinned, they will be forgiven. Therefore confess your sins to each other and pray for each other so that you may be healed. The prayer of a righteous person is powerful and effective. (James 5:13-16)

During my 180 journey, my pastor preached about Abraham praying for the cities of Sodom and Gomorrah to be spared for the sake of his nephew Lot, who lived there with his wife and daughters. The people of these two cities "were arrogant, overfed and unconcerned; they did not help the poor and needy. They were haughty and did detestable things" (Ezekiel 16:49,50). They "gave themselves up to sexual immorality and perversion" (Jude 7). God had rescued them from destruction once before, but they did not change their ways. When Abraham learned of God's plans to finally bring the people of these cities to justice, he started praying and asking God to spare the cities if there were 50 righteous people living there. God agreed to the request, but then Abraham started to haggle with God. Would God spare the cities if they had only 45 righteous people? only 40? only 30? only 20? Abraham continued his plea all the way down to ten righteous people. As it turned out, there were not even ten righteous people in the cities, but God was merciful and spared Lot and his daughters

(Genesis chapters 18,19). It's striking to me how God listens to us and takes our requests so seriously that the things we say to him have such a powerful effect. We are told that "the prayer of a righteous person is powerful and effective" (James 5:16).

As humans on this earth, we see only one aspect of life's situations and cares, but God sees the whole picture. Why should God get ideas from us about what to do? It's amazing to me that God still listens to us and promises to answer us the way he does. It gives me chills just thinking about it. He actually listens to us! But there is nothing to listen to if we are too shortsighted to talk to him.

Our human shortsightedness isn't the only reason God would have for not listening to us. There is also our sin. God says, "If anyone turns a deaf ear to my instruction, even their prayers are detestable" (Proverbs 28:9). Prayer is a gift to those who have faith in God. God does not listen to the prayers of the faithless. Who of us can say that we have never turned a deaf ear to God? Think how offensive it is to turn a deaf ear to the one who has loved us since before the world began. But God listens to believers. When we pray, Jesus prays too, asking his Father to hear us. "Christ Jesus who died—more than that, who was raised to life—is at the right hand of God and is also interceding for us" (Romans 8:34). For this intercession I am eternally thankful. This gift of prayer does not come from one ounce of our being. It comes from Jesus—Jesus, who never turned a deaf ear to God even when God asked him to die on the cross for the world. Because of Jesus' cross and Jesus' prayers, we can pray boldly and confidently. "This is the confidence we have in approaching God: that if we ask anything according to his will, he hears us. And if we know that he hears us—whatever we ask—we know that we have what we asked of him" (1 John 5:14,15). Thanks be to God for allowing us to pray to him, and thanks be to the Holy Spirit for helping us remember how important it is to communicate with our Savior from sin! As a nurse, I experience shortcomings in communication almost daily. I experience waiting for some sort of communication so that I can better take care of my patients. Through journaling about these shortcomings, I've begun to understand the importance of waiting on God in prayer and the amazing privilege prayer is.

TRAVEL TIPS: Prayer

Maybe you have experience with prayer—but maybe not. If prayer is new to you, it may feel awkward at first. So how do you pray?

↻ Pray daily as you journal. Prayer is your ability and privilege to talk to your Creator. Prayer is powerful. It's your direct line of communication with God. God speaks to you through the Bible, and you have the privilege to speak directly to God because of Jesus' sacrifice on the cross. How awesome is that! An important aspect of the 180 journey is daily prayer related to your topic. I learned a lot about prayer during my 180 journey. God will likely be changing your heart, attitude, perspective, etc., and what better way to digest these things than with prayer?

↻ Prayer does not need to be done on your knees at the side of your bed before you turn in for the night, the way it's often depicted in children's books. Prayer is an option all the time, and God wants you to talk to him about anything anywhere. You can pray when you're driving to the dentist, trying to find toothpicks at the grocery store, or walking into work. He is with you every step of the way, and you can pray to him at all times.

↻ What do you talk to him about? One aspect of prayer is asking God for help in a certain area of your life, whether asking for help in finding car keys, for patience at work, or for the healing of a family member with a serious illness. There is nothing too big or too small to ask for. Thinking either way puts God in a box.

↻ What God does tell you about asking him for things is that your motivation should be pure. "When you ask, you do not receive, because you ask with wrong motives, that you may spend what you get on your pleasures" (James 4:3).

↻ In addition to requests, I also thank God for various things that have happened to me and others: safe travels, health, home, food, etc. It's truly wowing when you start to thank God on a daily basis as you realize the day-to-day blessings in your life that could only be attributed to a gracious God. Repentance is another part of my prayer life.
I admit the wrongs I have done and ask God for forgiveness.
I have to admit that out of requests, thankfulness, and

repentance, I am the least consistent with repentance. But praying to God out of repentance and asking for forgiveness is such a special thing because you know that your sins *are* forgiven.

Friends Disappoint

It's common in life for people to let you down. Sometimes you wait and wait for an answer from someone, but it doesn't come. . . . Luckily for God, he doesn't get annoyed with us if we ask too many questions. In fact, he loves to hear from his children. Sometimes his answer though isn't what we want to hear, but it's a piece of the puzzle for his ultimate plan. [Day 11 of 180]

Have you ever been left hanging? You text friends about getting together, and they don't get back to you. Or when they do get back to you, it's too late to get together. It can be frustrating, especially if it's often the same people. I'll be the first one to admit to not texting back right away one hundred percent of the time, so I'm not in the clear. As frustrating as this can be, it's a good reminder to me that friends and family may disappoint, but God never leaves me hanging. Waiting on a friend's text isn't a sure thing; waiting on God is.

There is a section of scripture in the book of Matthew that gives me comfort that God always hears what I have to say even if the topic is seemingly minuscule. "Ask and it will be given to you; seek and you will find; knock and the door will be opened to you. For everyone who asks receives; the one who seeks finds; and to the one who knocks, the door will be opened" (Matthew 7:7,8). God will have a listening ear 24/7. He never goes on vacation, he never needs a break from his children, and he loves to hear from them. This is a realization I had on my 180 journey: As I saw the faults of others and myself, including unanswered phone calls and texts, I realized the perfection of Christ and the imperfection of the world.

Prayer is such a big part of waiting on God because of *what prayer is*. Prayer is not just talking to God; it is also counting on him to respond. It's counting on him to be there for you, give you the help you're asking for, and *show* you that he's listening.

A couple of Bible passages actually make the connection that waiting on friends doesn't always pay off, but waiting on God in prayer does. For example, see how the prophet Micah made that connection.

Do not trust a neighbor;
put no confidence in a friend.
Even with the woman who lies in your embrace
guard the words of your lips.
For a son dishonors his father,
a daughter rises up against her mother,
a daughter-in-law against her mother-in-law—
a man's enemies are the members of his own household.
But as for me, I watch in hope for the LORD,
I wait for God my Savior;
my God will hear me. (Micah 7:5-7)

Micah lived in very evil times. It is one thing to know that friends will sometimes let you down. It's something else altogether to live in fear and know that your spouse or your own child is ready to betray you and have you arrested because of your faith. I can hardly imagine that. Had Micah been betrayed by his own wife or children? He doesn't say. But he says he was waiting for God to keep him safe, counting on God to be his one trustworthy friend. For Micah, that all meant praying, "I wait for God my Savior; my God will hear me."

We have the same ideas as songwriter David in Psalm 38:11-15. He had no one to turn to when his life was in danger, but he knew he could turn to God in prayer. He knew that God would do more than just listen to him and sympathize with him. God would *answer* him. David said this was how he waited for God:

My friends and companions avoid me because
of my wounds;
my neighbors stay far away.
Those who want to kill me set their traps,
those who would harm me talk of my ruin;
all day long they scheme and lie.
LORD, I wait for you;
you will answer, Lord my God. (Psalm 38:11,12,15)

What a great blessing and comfort it is to know that we can pray to God and he hears us—and he answers! We are completely undeserving of this, but by God's grace we can go to his throne to make requests.

It's true that his answer may be "Not right now," "Wait," or "No, this isn't what is best for you," but he never forgets to call you back. In fact, God *wants* to hear from his children. Therefore, we should pray boldly, knowing one hundred percent that he will answer. If that answer is to wait, then pray for patience. Friends, family, and coworkers will disappoint. They fail to step in when expected, don't answer texts, and break promises. At worst, they even abandon, betray, or abuse. What a blessing it is that Jesus Christ has a perfect track record at making sure his Father answers people's prayers! Jesus promises, "Whoever comes to me I will never drive away" (John 6:37), and this promise is still true because "Jesus Christ is the same yesterday and today and forever" (Hebrews 13:8). Let's remember (me too) to go to God first, not last, because for Jesus' sake he will always be faithful.

TRAVEL TIPS: Commitment

Is 180 days attainable? Be real with yourself. When you set a goal, you want it to have a balance of being both challenging and attainable. If you think that 180 days is not attainable, maybe try 100 days. If it's too hard to commit to the weekends, perhaps try taking weekends off so it will end up being 180 weekdays. Do what makes sense in your life. However, I personally think that, at the very minimum, 50 days should be dedicated to this journey. After completing 180 days, I have learned more about waiting on God than I thought was possible.

Perfection: Ben's Work Mistake

One of the most agonizing things it seems is waiting for the score from the judges. Waiting to see what they did wrong, if they were "perfect" enough. [Day 51 of 180]

Yesterday, Ben didn't tell me about a mistake he had done. [Day 54 of 180]

God surprises me with his grace. He reminds me that no one is perfect, especially me as I fall so short of waiting on God. This is an unexpected conclusion I have gleaned from this little 180 journey.

Ben came home one night after work and was unusually quiet. Usually he's jovial, constantly trying to make me laugh and sometimes succeeding, but this night he was different. He said he was tired and wanted to relax by watching a television show. This is atypical of us as a couple. We don't watch much TV, let alone spend our evenings apart watching separate shows. But that night it seemed like he was just plain exhausted. I gave Ben the space he seemed to need. I know that at times Ben's job can be stressful with deadlines and dealing with contractors or architects. I guess that all comes with being a structural engineer. He's usually good at leaving work at work, but for whatever reason, it appeared that the stress caught up to him that night. We normally tell each other everything, so I didn't think of it being anything more than everyday work stress.

The next day I found out the real reason behind Ben's off behavior. He told me that he had made an error at work the day before and realized it at the end of the day. All night he seemed quiet and tired, but in reality, he had this mistake on his mind, trying to come up with a cost-effective solution. As a structural engineer, if he makes mistakes in his work, it could mean a detrimental event if the building is already built or is in the process of being built and the problem hasn't been caught by anyone else. The absolute worst-case scenario is that the building could fall and people could be injured or even die. Realizing his error, Ben got to work early the next morning and was able to come up with a relatively easy solution to the problem he had created. Although I was happy for him that he was able to work out a simple solution, it bothered me that he had kept this from me the night it occurred. Did he think he'd disappoint me? Did he not want me to worry? We talked about this issue that night, and it turns out it was a little bit of both. He promised he wouldn't keep things like this from me again.

As hurt as I was that Ben didn't come to me for help or a listening ear, God probably is more hurt when he sees his children in pain and sees them go to empty wells attempting to fill themselves up and never being satisfied. We turn to TV, alcohol, or friends and family rather than to God. I don't always turn to the Creator, who knows and understands what's hurting before I even mumble the words to him. Psalm 139:4 says, "Before a word is on my tongue you, LORD, know it completely." God clearly says in his Word to rely completely on him. "I wait for the LORD, my whole being waits, and in his word I put my hope. I wait for the Lord more than watchmen wait for the morning, more than watchmen wait for the morning" (Psalm 130:5,6). The verses here emphasize waiting on the Lord with one's "whole being." God doesn't want me waiting on him only when it feels right or makes me feel or look good, but, rather, with one hundred percent of my being one hundred percent of the time.

In this world, it is just plain inevitable that we are going to make mistakes. We are not perfect. Human beings were created to be perfect, but Adam and Eve messed it up by sinning in the Garden of Eden. Let's face it—it could have been any one of us sinning in the garden. Since we all are sinful, we all let one another down. I especially learned through my 180 journey how many times I failed at waiting on God. I did not lean on him with one hundred percent of my being. I tried to handle things myself and did what I felt was best for me.

Perfection: The Olympics

Another place I noticed an emphasis on perfection that can never be obtained is the Olympics. Ben and I love watching the Olympics on TV. We binge-watched the Summer Olympics in 2016. Like I mentioned before, we aren't big TV watchers, so our TV is not in our living room but in our spare bedroom instead. However, during the Olympics we make an exception and set up the TV in our living room. We especially enjoy watching the gymnastics and swimming events. I noticed that one of the most agonizing things for the athletes is waiting for the final score from the judges. It's crazy to think that all the years the athletes have trained come down to this one moment. After each performance, the cameras are on the athletes, who often are breathing hard, trying to recover from their event. They are waiting to see what they did wrong, if they were perfect enough, and are likely replaying their performances in their heads.

God doesn't judge performances like an Olympic judge. He judges our souls. We can strive for perfection, but there's no way we can ever reach his expectations. "Whoever keeps the whole law and yet stumbles at just one point is guilty of breaking all of it" (James 2:10). We all falter and sin, but thankfully God sees his Son's perfection when he sees us. "It is by grace you have been saved, through faith—and this is not from yourselves, it is the gift of God—not by works, so that no one can boast" (Ephesians 2:8,9).

It's crazy how God still loves careless sinners. He still loves Ben even after a work mistake. God still loved Adam and Eve. And God still loves Steph, even after my countless failures to wait on him. We sinners are completely undeserving of his grace, and we should show thankfulness to God for it. We instantly have his grace; there is no waiting period to receive or earn it. It's already paid for and done. Through journaling and reflecting on waiting on God more, I have become more thankful and mindful of how great and immediate this blessing really is.

YOUR TURN: 180

My hope from you reading about my 180 journey thus far is that it inspires you to do the same in your life. There may be many different reasons you would choose to do a 180 (remember, 180 refers not only to 180 days or six months but more importantly to a distinct and tangible change, perhaps even a complete 180-degree change).

My topic for 180 days was waiting on God more. You may choose this topic or another topic, such as loving God more or trusting God more, that may be more fitting for you. Choose a topic that you are either passionate about or challenged by. Before diving in, plan to have the following in place:

- Pray about it: Have you talked to God yet about your big plans of dedicating extra time to him for 180 days? Pray for perseverance and dedication during this time of really diving into God's Word.

- Connect with an accountability partner.

- Buy a fresh journal or begin a new digital journal on your laptop or tablet.

- Put up reminders of whatever you are studying. I put reminders of waiting on God more on my bathroom mirror and my nightstand. These reminders could be Bible passages or personal notes to keep you focused.

Why 180? I think the motivation is probably different for each person. Below are a few reasons. Perhaps your reasoning is a combination of some of these:

- To deepen a belief in a Bible teaching you already know is true.

- To find an answer in an area about which you have some doubt or uncertainty.

- To tackle some part of your faith life that you feel is hypocritical.

- To build a deeper relationship with God.

Waiting on God Means Not Getting So Hung up on What I Don't Have

Close Call

It's easy to wait on God for obvious things in your life that you can see, feel, and observe. But imagine all the things you don't see. I thought about this recently on my ride home from work. I made a last-minute chiropractor appointment immediately following my shift at the hospital because my neck had been bothering me. After my chiropractor appointment, I was driving home, and Ben called me saying there had just been an accident on the main freeway I take home from work, minutes away from my exit. He called to give me a heads-up about the traffic so that I could take an alternative route.

On my drive home, I was thinking more about that accident. The time the accident occurred is normally when I would be in that same location on my commute home from work. Thankfully, because of my last-minute chiropractor appointment, I completely bypassed it all. I could have been in that car accident—it was so bad that it shut down both sides of the freeway. I could have been in that accident where Flight for Life had to be called in. God was looking out for me that day. It was easy that day to complain about my sore neck instead of remembering to wait on God. It seems as though God would have said, "How about if I use your sore neck to keep you out of that Flight for Life helicopter?"

When I was reflecting about this close call with Ben over dinner that night, he replied, "Doesn't it make you think of all the times that you have been in harm's way but didn't even know it? All the times God has kept us safe even though seconds before or after could have been disastrous?"

Ben is so right. It's easy to thank God when a near-death experience happens before your eyes, but what about all those times you don't even know what you don't know when it comes to God intervening and protecting you?

God is always looking after me, even though I do not deserve it. I don't think to thank him for all the times he has kept me safe and has sent his angels to look after me. I just take for granted that God's strength will be there and he will look after me. I truly do not understand the magnitude of how much he has kept me safe. When it comes to waiting on God, Christians often do not even know what to expect or what to ask for. But thankfully God intercedes for us and keeps us safe and works out what is best to further his kingdom.

God Provides

I didn't even have time to "wait on God," He simply provided what I needed. Like a shepherd who gives their sheep what they need. [Day 2 of 180]

One thing I noticed that changed in my 180 journey is that when I first started, I was often more retrospective. I would settle down to journal right before bed, and it was then that I would go through my day, narrowing down the ways God had shone through. For example, the ways he provided and the ways I waited on him or fell short and didn't wait on him. The couple of sentences above are straight from my journal, only the second entry. For those first tries, I reflected at the end of the day, running a comb through that day's events and trying to find ways I was waiting on God. But by the end of my 180 experience, I found myself instinctively and purposefully reflecting throughout the day. It certainly was not perfectly straightforward or easy, but I was growing, getting better at noticing the lessons and blessings in each moment of life.

Often God doesn't give you what you want, but he does give you what you need. God has blessed me more than I can imagine. I eat until I am satisfied, and when I'm done, I still have enough food left in my pantry and chest freezer to last me a couple of months. God has blessed me with a job that I find edifying where I have the privilege to care for people. He's blessed Ben and me with two working cars, and he gives us the means to fix them as needed. He recently gave us a house and all the unnecessary things in the house that make a home cozy. He has given overall health to my family and me. He has given me all these things, but why do I find it so easy to complain about whatever is not perfectly aligned in my life? "The Lord is my shepherd, I lack nothing" (Psalm 23:1). What a great reminder God gives to us: Because of Christ's grace, his people truly lack nothing.

Instead of thinking how hard it is to wait for God to fix the latest broken part of my life, I can take the time and notice a few hundred more of the happinesses he has already given me.

Mononucleosis

Happy Thanksgiving . . . and 8th day of being sick. Wait for it . . . with mono. Yes, mono. Who would have thought? I got the phone call from my doctor Sunday night. I was shocked to say the least. But it makes sense because usually I'm sick for a day, maybe two. [Day 119 of 180]

I thought I was a patient person until I became sick with mononucleosis (mono). I have a somewhat unusual immune system in which I can get rid of a cold as fast as I come down with one. I take vitamins and tea when I feel the start of a cold coming on, when my throat begins to feel scratchy and my nose is stuffy. On average, I'm sick only about half a day to a full day, perhaps two days at most. When this cold quickly came on but then lingered for three days without any signs of getting better, I finally went to see the doctor. I was having fevers, chills, severe exhaustion, and the worst sore throat. The doctor took one good look at my swollen and spotted tonsils and immediately ordered a blood test for mono. I was surprised when it came back positive. Ironically, I was similar to the patients I deal with at work: in denial of how sick I really was. Mono is caused by the Epstein-Barr virus, which an antibiotic is not able to fight. Since there are no medications that cure mono, my doctor said to "ride it out" by drinking lots of fluids and resting. On top of severe exhaustion, a sore throat, fevers, and chills, I developed an awful cough. It's not very typical to get a cough with mono, so my doctor said I was likely fighting multiple viruses at the same time. This cough was the type that keeps you up at night: dry, hacking, persistent. I went through at least four bags of cough drops that week.

Ben was so wonderful during the time I was sick. He took on all the housework, including grocery shopping and making sure I always had enough soup and popsicles. In addition, he stayed home with me on Thanksgiving and made us a complete holiday dinner, since I couldn't attend our families' gatherings. Ben went all out: Cornish hens, sweet potatoes, stuffing, cranberry sauce, pecan pie, and apple pie. Yes, he baked two types of pie for just the two of us. I can't think of many husbands who would go through all the work of making a Thanksgiving dinner.

Ben has a servant's heart and shows his love to me daily, but he isn't one to bring home flowers. In fact, I think he has only bought me flowers three times in all the years we have been together. But one act of love that Ben does frequently is making me fancy dinners on special nights, complete with candlelight. He loves to cook and I love to eat, so it's the perfect combination. Not to mention that it's fantastic quality time, which is important to both of us.

But there was another way Ben helped my Thanksgiving attitude. He suggested I write down 20 things I was thankful for. I had been a bit down about feeling sick and missing the dinners with family, so this seemed like the reminder I needed. It really didn't take long at all. I could have gone on for pages! Here it is, straight from my 180 journal:

1. Jesus, who selflessly took my place and died for me
2. Family—both blood and those married in (I have awesome in-laws)
3. Friends—they feel like family
4. Our lovely new home
5. Things to look forward to, like the new *Gilmore Girls* being released
6. Ben—enough said
7. A job where I make a difference every day
8. Cough drops—they're the only reason I can (kind of) sleep right now
9. Hot tea
10. Electric blankets
11. The ability to make modifications to our home
12. Health—being sick has reminded me to not take it for granted
13. Our food every day—especially the Thanksgiving food Ben is making
14. My niece—we nearly lost her this year and she brings so much joy
15. The ease of mind, knowing that now we can start a family— God willing
16. Freedom in America
17. Veterans for risking/sacrificing their life

18. Chocolate
19. Camp Phillip
20. The freedom that we are able to vote for who we'd like
    in America

I needed to make a list like that because despite all the love being shown to me by Ben and family and friends during this time I was sick, I still managed to complain plenty. I was becoming increasingly impatient. I felt exhausted from simply walking to the kitchen to make myself tea. I felt useless because all I could do was eat, sleep, and watch movies. I didn't want to wait anymore for God to make me better. Even when I started to feel a little better, I would still tire out so quickly. My mind thought I could do something simple like the dishes, but after a couple of minutes my body was exhausted and I needed to lie back down. This was frustrating to me: to feel decent while in bed but unable to do anything physical.

Having mono and basically being bedridden for 11 days made me rely on God more, constantly relying on him for peace and healing and, in general, just talking with him. God wants us to be joyful (to glory) in our sufferings as he tells us in Paul's letter to the Romans, "We also glory in our sufferings, because we know that suffering produces perseverance; perseverance, character; and character, hope" (Romans 5:3,4). Mono took my patience to the next level. I was definitely talking to God more and relying on his Word and wisdom. As each new day brought more sickness, my attitude grew closer and closer to the attitude of waiting that David expressed in Psalm 5:3.

In the morning, LORD, you hear my voice;
in the morning I lay my requests before you
and wait expectantly.

I relied on my favorite Bible passage to calm me: "The LORD will fight for you; you need only to be still" (Exodus 14:14). I couldn't fight this on my own. Not an ounce of worrying could help the situation. This Bible passage was the reminder I needed of my complete dependence on God, and it ended up being something I took great comfort in.

And guess what? Other than some mild exhaustion for a few weeks after being sick, I did not have any long-lasting effects. Mono is a comparatively minor illness, and the majority of people recover. It is also something you typically only get once. I do not have a lifelong disease I am battling (although latent Lyme cannot be ruled out, but I am symptom free at the moment). That in and of itself is something to be thankful for. Also, Ben did not end up catching mono, which was a huge blessing. I can't even imagine how much more difficult my recovery would have been if Ben had been sick too. (Not to mention how terrible it would have been for him!)

Reflecting back, I am also thankful for a job with sick leave so that I could call in sick for a number of days without issue (and still get paid!). That brings me to one last lesson I learned from having mono: Once again God showed me that his timing is inherently perfect. Back in July when I had had to place vacation requests at work for the fall and winter, I randomly asked off the first week in December. Ben and I had talked about vacationing somewhere that week, but we ended up deciding not to go anywhere. We were just going to enjoy life in our new home and get ready for the quickly approaching holidays. Deciding not to travel anywhere that week was a godsend! God blessed me with one full bonus week off from work after being sick from mono. Only God knows how much I needed that week! I never could have predicted back in July that I would need additional time off in December to recover from mono, but God knew.

YOUR TURN

- Are you currently waiting for something joyful to happen: getting married, having a baby, moving into your new home? Or are you waiting for something that is a tough situation: lab results, a meeting with the principal of your troubled teen, an expensive bill from the hospital?

- How can you praise God during the trials and triumphs in your life?

- Challenge: Set a timer for ten minutes and list as many things as you can that you are thankful for.

    - Are you surprised by how many items you listed?

    - Idea: Hang this list somewhere in your home where it can remind you of all the blessings in your life.

- Search for Bible passages that have the word *wait* in them with a concordance or online search engine like biblegateway.com. Skim through the list and find some passages that encourage waiting on God. Pick two or three that hit home for you, write them down, and reflect on them. Journaling may help your thoughts about those passages become even clearer as you force yourself to put them into words.

Ticking Time Bombs

Sometimes in life we are waiting for good things, while other times we are holding our breath in anticipation of something bad happening. At work my patients are not always waiting for something positive. We sometimes use the phrase "ticking time bombs" in nurse-to-nurse, change-of-shift reports. It's not a very pleasant image, but it gets the point across when we are trying to convey quickly and effectively to the oncoming nurse how labile (or unstable) a patient's medical condition currently is. One patient I took care of was a man with a large hematoma on his kidney, and he was a ticking time bomb. He could have hemorrhaged at an alarming rate, requiring emergency surgery or multiple blood transfusions. He could have died at literally any second. It was scary for me to care for him and even scarier for the patient. Surprisingly, he was walking around without any outward symptoms or even pain. This was almost more alarming for the patient, and for me caring for him, because he likely wouldn't have shown any obvious signs of his health quickly spiraling out of control.

We are all ticking time bombs in our own way. We are all born destined for hell, ticking away until we die. If we don't know or believe what the Bible says about sin, we are walking around as if everything is fine, but it isn't. Thankfully, with Christ's sacrifice of dying and taking away all our sins, we are washed clean from sin. Because of this truth, we do not need to worry if we've done enough to make it into heaven. Jesus has taken care of it. He has diffused the bomb, and we can live free of fear.

Every Day Is a Bonus

Sometimes you need to experience how fleeting time really, truly is and that it is a gift. For example, the average working person works first shift Monday through Friday and has off Saturday and Sunday. That is not always the case when you work at a hospital. There will always be sick people who need to be cared for, and health-care workers need to cover the 24/7 care needs of these patients. I've grown accustomed to working every other weekend. Some weekends it's harder going into work than others depending on what I am missing that day, whether it's a niece's birthday party or a last-minute barbeque at the lake.

One Saturday that I was scheduled to work, I did not have any plans, but I knew it was going to be a gorgeous day, a high of 74 degrees and sunny. It was the first warm day that we'd had in a long time. The other reason I wasn't excited about working this particular Saturday was because I was feeling a little bit under the weather, trying to get over a cold. Reluctantly I walked into work that morning. Then the charge nurse told me, "Steph, you won the lottery! You get to go home if you'd like!" I gathered my things and walked right out of there!

I celebrated by buying too much food at a favorite local bakery and surprised Ben with breakfast on the patio. After our leisurely breakfast, I opened up all the windows in the house and went to work cleaning the dishes and folding the laundry that I'd been putting off for a few days. In the afternoon, I gardened and then relaxed on the patio. This Saturday felt sweeter than my usual weekend off. It could have been the weather and the good food that pointed my day in this direction, but it felt so good to savor this time at home and this time of rest, which I knew I never should have had in the first place!

As I pondered my Saturday off from work that shouldn't have happened, I wondered what would happen if I entered every day with this sort of appreciative attitude. I would likely live more intentionally and boldly, knowing that each day was an undeserved and unexpected gift!

That reminds me of something I heard once that has always stuck with me: Every day is a bonus.

Have you ever heard of the Honor Flight Network? It's a nonprofit organization that began in 2005 whose goal is to show appreciation to veterans for their service in the military. Its mission: "To celebrate America's veterans by inviting them to share in a day of honor at our nation's memorials." In 2016 alone, it flew out 20,558 veterans, giving them the opportunity to be paid well-deserved honor and respect. Honor Flight started out serving World War II veterans, trying to give every living World War II veteran the opportunity to see their war memorial that was completed in 2004. Today the organization continues to serve World War II veterans and has expanded to both Korean War and Vietnam War veterans, as well as any terminally ill veterans. Ben's Grandpa, "Goompa" as we called him, was able to see the World War II memorial as part of an Honor Flight in 2012 before he passed away in 2013. The group of veterans had a large welcome home ceremony at the Milwaukee Mitchell International Airport after a long day of visiting memorials in Washington, D.C. Our family made sure to be there. It was moving to see those veterans with tears streaming down their faces, pondering the day's events and moved by the love and support that was outpoured to them. For some veterans, especially the Vietnam veterans, they may not have experienced gratitude or support upon returning home from war. This time, however, the crowd was decked out in red, white, and blue. There were patriotic songs blasted by high school bands, countless handmade signs, and tons of cheering. There were so many emotions: gratitude for the veterans who had sacrificed so much of their lives for their country, joy that the veterans were receiving the thanks they deserved, and sadness for hardships and losses they may have faced while serving our country. I felt so honored to be there to welcome the veterans home.

In December 2012, the documentary *Honor Flight* was released. I highly recommend seeing it. A word of caution: Don't be caught without a box of tissues. This documentary follows the lives of various veterans before, during, and after the Honor Flight. You hear many statements from the veterans like, "It was the best day of my life!" One of the quotes from the movie that always sticks with me is "Every day is a bonus." This was originally said by Joe Demler, a World War II Army private who was a prisoner of war held by the Germans. Many of his fellow prisoners passed away from starvation, and when he was finally liberated from the

Nazi prison camp, he weighed a mere 70 pounds. A photo of him taken that day was published in many magazines, and he became known as "the human skeleton." His chances of recovering were slim, but he did recover. And later when he told reporters of his time in the prison camp, he said, "I learned to pray and I learned that *every day is a bonus.*"

None of us know if we will be here on this earth tomorrow; only God knows. He says, "Do not boast about tomorrow, for you do not know what a day may bring" (Proverbs 27:1). Can you imagine seeing hell on this earth and being at death's door and still having a positive outlook? Every day I am blessed because the veterans I work with—veterans who are a lot like Joe Demler—inspire me. They knock me down a few pegs (in a good way) from my lofty, idealistic, and comfortable life. They know what it's like to be a number, to be stripped of identity, family, and belongings. They also understand what it means to be brave, what it means to have brothers who are not blood related, what it means to have given it their all. These men are true heroes.

In his Word, God gives us instructions on how our valuable time should be spent: "Be very careful, then, how you live—not as unwise but as wise, making the most of every opportunity, because the days are evil" (Ephesians 5:15,16). Every breath could be our last; we really don't know. Every extra day we live is a gift, and God tells us to use it wisely, "making the most of every opportunity, because the days are evil."

Instead of living each and every day worrying about day-to-day life happenings, I can strive to live joyfully because every day is a bonus, not because I have survived starvation in a prison camp but because I know this is my time of grace. Are you familiar with that phrase? Grace is what fills God's heart. It is his desire to do good, kind, and generous things for his people, not because they've earned it but just because he likes to. We have each been given a time of grace here on earth. Our lives are a time to learn God's grace and to learn how kind and generous he is, especially in sending us Jesus. Our lives are also a time to help others learn God's grace, a time here on this earth to preach that good news of God's love and kindness to all creation. A time to live as Jesus lived: boldly, without fear, and with love. I recently read a quote that sums up our role in the world perfectly:

We are on a journey to become a church that does what matters most by obeying the Great Commandment (to love God and our neighbor; Matt. 22:36-40), the Great Compassion (to serve the least; Matt. 25:31-46), and the Great Commission (to make disciples; Matt. 28:18-20). The world is hungry for real, authentic love. (Brian Mavis and Rick Rusaw, *The Neighboring Church: Getting Better at What Jesus Says Matters Most*, Thomas Nelson Publishers, 2016, Kindle file)

My prayer is that you don't have to do a 180 journey to realize this but that you realize this here with me now and join me in boldly living each day for Christ in thought, word, and action. Through my 180 journey, I realized that I often forgot this truth—that every day on this earth truly is a bonus because God can take away my earthly life at any moment. I feel like I have so much more to wait on God for. I need to recognize the bonuses he has already given me.

Miracles

Often, you need to see the absence of something to fully appreciate the miracle taking place. I was pretty sick last week, and now I feel well and I appreciate it even more and think about my health and am grateful for my health even more. [Day 71 of 180]

God often sets his people up for miracles, arranging the circumstances so that the wonder of the miracle really gets noticed.

For example, remember the feeding of the five thousand. If you have not read it recently, go ahead and look it up in Matthew 14:13-21. Jesus had his disciples look at their food supply before he performed the miracle. He challenged them, "You give them something to eat." He made a point of showing them there were only five loaves of bread and two fish. That way it was all the more impressive when he used that little lunchbox to feed the crowd of thousands of people—yes, and to feed them until they were completely satisfied. They even had 12 basketfuls of leftovers!

Feeding five thousand people from a few loaves of bread and fish is a true miracle. A miracle by definition is an act that is not explained by known laws of nature, a supernatural act. It defied human logic, and the laws of nature were bent when Jesus fed five thousand people out of basically nothing. In my life, I try to notice as many of God's wonders as I can, just like the disciples witnessed the miracle of feeding the five thousand. Often, however, I need to be threatened with the absence of something to fully appreciate God's wonders taking place. I am thankful for health after a bout of sickness. I am thankful for family after a family scare happens and the threat of losing someone becomes a reality. I am more thankful for my husband when I see another married couple who are suffering. I am thankful for our home after it barely missed damage from a severe storm.

There have been many other times that my thankfulness needed prompting. We all forget to be thankful sometimes. For example, Ben had to show me the extensive yard work he did all day that I failed to notice when I pulled in the driveway. I didn't take the time to be thankful. If Ben grabbed a snack from the pantry and didn't notice that I had completely reorganized it earlier that day, he didn't take the time to be thankful. Thankfulness ensues only after the act has been pointed out. As an imperfect human, I often need to be prompted, I need my eyes to be opened, and I sometimes even need to be hit upside the head in order to notice what is right in front of me.

God understands our imperfections, our distractedness, and our tendency to take everyone, including him, for granted.

I think another great example of God setting up the situation to exemplify his power is the story of Gideon and his army in Judges chapter 7. Gideon had an army of 32,000 soldiers that God decreased to 10,000. That was still too many, so God dwindled the army from 10,000 to a mere 300 soldiers. God was proving a point here:

> The LORD said to Gideon, "You have too many men. I cannot deliver Midian into their hands, or Israel would boast against me, 'My own strength has saved me.'" (Judges 7:2)

When Gideon and his small army of only three hundred soldiers landed a win just like God had promised, they couldn't help but think that this win was given to them by the strength of the one above rather than the strength of their army. God set this scene up dramatically. It sounds crazy for a commander to send home soldiers right before an attack. But God can defy logic and can win a war of any kind by his power.

Through my 180 journey, I've noticed that God has to be over the top at times with the lessons he wants to teach me about waiting on him more, much like the way he "sets up" these miracles. I shouldn't need hardships in my surroundings to prompt me to thank God. I should be thanking God for my health every day, not just after my health is found to be fragile. Sickness can and does bring people closer to God, but I don't want it to turn into the only reason I'm seeking Jesus. I want to be better at waiting on God by not always depending on life's circumstances. Rather, I want to wait on God all the time, even when he does not give me an obvious "nudge" in his direction. I noticed that the further along I got on my journey, the less I required such prompting from God on what he was teaching me. My goal, through the help of God, is to be more observant of his wonders around me.

Patience

Often I feel like I am constantly in a state of waiting at work.
[Day 68 of 180]

I'm always waiting at work. Waiting for the doctor to put in discharge orders. Waiting for the IV team to call me back. Waiting for my patient to come back from an appointment. God tests my patience every day but especially at work.

On one particular workday, God tested my patience in a different way. I had to care for a patient who was mean and rude. This patient wore me down emotionally and physically. He spit in my direction when I tried to give him medications; he yelled at me to leave the room; he threatened to leave the hospital because we weren't helping him anyway. Many not-so-nice thoughts sneaked into my head in response to him. Thankfully none of them made it out of my mouth. Now, just because I was, with God's help, able to keep my mouth shut, that doesn't mean that I was perfect. I thought those hurtful and impatient responses, and God saw my thoughts. They were very ugly to him. Impatience that despises other people is ugly to God, whether it's out of my mouth or in my mind. Jesus said, "Anyone who is angry with a brother or sister will be subject to judgment" (Matthew 5:22). He says that "love is patient . . . it is not easily angered" (1 Corinthians 13:4,5). My feelings toward that patient just weren't love, and God saw that. God says, "Brothers and sisters, whatever is true, whatever is noble, whatever is right, whatever is pure, whatever is lovely, whatever is admirable—if anything is excellent or praiseworthy—think about such things" (Philippians 4:8).

God wants us to love our enemies. That seems completely opposite of what the world tells us in movies, TV shows, commercials, etc. The natural attitude is to get back at the person who was mean to you. Phrases like "He had it coming, acting that way" are thrown around to make it sound more acceptable. It seems almost abnormal not to retaliate and get even with the person who wronged you. But Jesus tells us to be abnormal like that:

> You have heard that it was said: "Love your neighbor and
> hate your enemy." But I tell you, love your enemies and

pray for those who persecute you, that you may be children of your Father in heaven. He causes his sun to rise on the evil and the good, and sends rain on the righteous and the unrighteous. If you love those who love you, what reward will you get? Are not even the tax collectors doing that? And if you greet only your own people, what are you doing more than others? Do not even pagans do that? Be perfect, therefore, as your heavenly Father is perfect. (Matthew 5:43-48)

Further, God tells us how to treat those whom we consider our enemies:

Love must be sincere. Hate what is evil; cling to what is good. Be devoted to one another in love. Honor one another above yourselves. Bless those who persecute you; bless and do not curse. Do not be proud, but be willing to associate with people of low position. Do not be conceited. Do not repay anyone evil for evil. Do not take revenge, my dear friends. . . . On the contrary: "If your enemy is hungry, feed him; if he is thirsty, give him something to drink. In doing this, you will heap burning coals on his head." Do not be overcome by evil, but overcome evil with good. (Romans 12:9,10,14,16,17,19-21)

Overcoming evil with good sounds like a tall order, doesn't it? Like I said before, the world communicates that people should get even with their enemies, not shower them with love. I needed to learn, and am still learning, what it means to wait on God to help me love those who are just plain hard to love.

Waiting is simply a part of life. Of course, some waiting challenges our patience more, like when it comes to being patient with those challenging people in our lives who make it much harder to love. Jesus set the example of living a perfect life without sin and being loving and kind to everyone. And what's more, he did all of this in our place so that we are credited with his righteousness. Jesus wasn't just the perfect example; he is our righteousness.

To this you were called, because Christ suffered for you, leaving you an example, that you should follow in his steps.

"He committed no sin,
and no deceit was found in his mouth."

When they hurled their insults at him, he did not retaliate; when he suffered, he made no threats. Instead, he entrusted himself to him who judges justly. "He himself bore our sins" in his body on the cross, so that we might die to sins and live for righteousness; "by his wounds you have been healed." For "you were like sheep going astray," but now you have returned to the Shepherd and Overseer of your souls. (1 Peter 2:21-25)

Either I can satisfy my sinful nature and come up with excuses about how annoying some people are and how they always rub me the wrong way, or I can act like a child of God who aspires to love. Lord, help each of us emulate your unconditional love. We truly only love because you first loved us. Help us remember this in everything we do. Amen.

YOUR TURN

- Is there someone in your life who makes it particularly challenging to show God's love?
- What are some other Bible passages you can find on loving your enemy?
- What are ways in which you can love those who are difficult to love?

Veterans Day

Happy Veterans Day! Happy to have served those who served.
Today I got pills spit at, a used wipe thrown at me, cussed at,
and kicked/hit by a confused patient. [Day 114 of 180]

My husband always says, "Wow, Veterans Day must feel like Christmas," referring to the times I get to work at the Veterans Affairs (VA) Hospital on Veterans Day. I never know exactly how to respond to that. In general, yes, there is a sort of joy in the air. Handmade Veterans Day cards are passed around to the patients from the local grade schools. Sometimes bands come in and play for the patients in the hospital or the residents in the nursing home. There is always some sort of Veterans Day service in the auditorium. But you can sometimes see in the patients' eyes that they are remembering. They can do a pretty good job of "forgetting" most days of the year, but this one day they are forced to remember—remember the good and the bad. For me, it doesn't change how I go about my day very much because I've gotten into the habit of thanking veterans for their service every day, not just on Veterans Day.

On this Veterans Day, however, I was having a rough day. I had a patient with advanced dementia who was confused and scared, and his defense was to act out. He spit out all his pills at me. (Thankfully he missed.) He cursed at me, and he attempted to kick and hit me many times. To say it was an exhausting day is an understatement.

I remember attending a family party immediately after this tiring workday. I was asked how my day at work had gone, and in reply I reported all the negative things I mentioned above, happy to have a sympathetic ear. Sometimes it's easy to share the frustrating parts of my job, but sharing joys about my job should come just as easily.

Reflecting later that evening, I realized I had only complained about my day. I had failed to mention the positive encounter I had had with this patient toward the end of my shift. Instead of telling him to do tasks like roll on your side, take your pills, or eat your breakfast, I decided on a different approach. I asked him about his military service. His whole demeanor changed. He talked about how he was in the Navy Reserves and once "crossed the equator 26 times, in one day!" I thanked him for his service and told him it was Veterans Day. He thought I was lying, so I gave him one of the handmade cards that children from the local grade school had made. He threw it back at me, and it fell to the floor. I guess you can't win them all.

I continued to care for this patient for many more days, and each time I made a point to talk to him as a person. Sometimes it was the same conversation about his military experience, but sometimes he would share things about his family or the job he had worked at for many years before he retired. The Bible says, "We love because he first loved us" (1 John 4:19). It's easier to say that than it is to act on it. I need reminders in my life, like this patient with dementia, to show me that everyone needs a little love. These people might have an impossibly hard facade to break. Their actions make them less lovable. But if we wait, God may let our love win through.

Time and time again, God shows me his grace—that generous heart of his. Sometimes I'm not searching for his grace, but it is what I need. I've noticed through my 180 journey that he shows me his grace through my patients every day, meaning I notice all the ways I fall short of showing his grace to my patients at times. The times I do remember his grace, I am very much encouraged to pass on a bit of it.

The Last Straw

> The bikes on the driveway. That was enough to set the man off as he pulled in from a stressful day of work. But it wasn't really the bikes. He accidentally overslept this morning and was late for work for the second time that week. He was tired because he didn't sleep well the night before, because he couldn't stop thinking about the garage door that doesn't quite close all the way. And then did he remember to put a towel under the leaking dishwasher before going to bed? And then came the news that the children need braces, $7,000 worth of them spread out over 18 months. Where is he going to get money for that when the garage door and the dishwasher need to be repaired? No, it wasn't just the bikes. It's just been a day for him. A week at least, maybe even a month. (adapted from Pastor Steinbrenner's sermon from Peace Lutheran in Hartford, WI)

This sermon really struck me. I hadn't been feeling well with being pregnant, so sometimes I took out my frustration on Ben. One day I had had an exhausting day at work with demanding and rude family members of my patients. Once home, I felt frustrated that the kitchen sink was overflowing with dishes from the night before that I didn't do because I was feeling sick. So I snapped at Ben. When Ben and I argue, he likes to find the root of every problem and talk about that root until we're both blue in the face. That got me more upset. Why couldn't he just take my crabbiness? Doesn't he know I don't feel well, I had a crummy day at work, and the house is a mess? Doesn't he notice these things? Instead, he was making me do all this extra talking, which made me even more frustrated. Snap. It's not just the bikes in the driveway; it's the day and its events.

I should have been focusing on the joyous fact that I was pregnant instead of waiting for the nausea to finally go away. I should have been focusing on the fact that I had a great job that serves people instead of focusing on how nasty people can be. I should have been focusing on the fact that having a sink overflowing with dishes meant Ben and I had plenty of food to fill our stomachs. I should have been focusing on the fact that Ben wants to get at the root cause of things because he cares about us and our relationship.

Day-to-day mishaps pile up. Some could even be categorized as major crises. Where does one turn? We turn to Jesus and his love so we can show that love to others.

Often when I feel stressed and overwhelmed by life, I fail to show love and patience like Jesus does. As sinful humans, we act on our feelings and emotions, but Jesus is perfect and while he was here on this earth, he never once lashed out. He never let the little things get to him. Because he suffered for us, we are called to do great things. "To this you were called, because Christ suffered for you, leaving you an example, that you should follow in his steps. 'He committed no sin, and no deceit was found in his mouth'" (1 Peter 2:21,22). Can you imagine being Jesus and watching the people you created constantly sinning and even preaching against you? I'm thankful to Jesus that he led a perfect life so I wouldn't have to. There's no way I could lead a perfect life because "surely I was sinful at birth, sinful from the time my mother conceived me" (Psalm 51:5). When Adam and Eve sinned in the Garden of Eden thousands of years ago, sin entered the world. Every person who has entered the world since then entered the world sinful and in dire need of the Savior, who would sacrifice his life on the cross for the sins of all people from all time.

Instead of acting in anger, God wants me to show compassion. Instead of assuming the worst in people, God wants me to assume the best. Instead of letting the little things in life pile up and create worry, unhealthy stress, and shrinking faith, God wants me to put my full reliance and trust in him. God wants me to love others because he loved me first.

Whoever does not love does not know God, because God is love. This is how God showed his love among us: He sent his one and only Son into the world that we might live through him. This is love: not that we loved God, but that he loved us and sent his Son as an atoning sacrifice for our sins. Dear friends, since God so loved us, we also ought to love one another. (1 John 4:8-11)

I've learned through my 180 journey that I often let the small stuff bother me. I worry about circumstances that are completely out of my control. The devil is sneaky and uses the small mishaps in life to throw me for a loop and cause me to fall into sin. He piles the problems up to funnel anger into my life, to get me to assume the worst of others, and then I'm causing divisions. I need God's help when I'm trying to be patient with difficult people at work. I need God's help when I'm waiting for money to come in to pay off bills. I need God's help when I'm waiting for necessary house repairs to be done. I need God's help in a relationship that doesn't seem to grow. This is where the love of God spoken of in 1 John chapter 4 comes in. It's a sweet, sweet, and unfathomable grace. This grace washes over all the times I let my earthly pile of problems engulf me, the pile that leads me to take out my frustrations on Ben. My sin is why I need God's love, and his grace is why I want to show his love.

Noah

Yesterday, Ben and I read about Noah and his ark. Can you imagine waiting for it to stop raining (40 days) and then waiting around for the land to dry up—waiting for an olive branch. I would have been very crabby I think—a smelly ark with not much ventilation and probably the same food every day! God doesn't really tell us that Noah complained at all. In fact, Noah praises God and makes an altar in thanksgiving. It was the first thing he did. I'd probably want to run all around and satisfy myself with freedom, sunshine, and fresh air and run around and stretch my legs. My first inkling would be far from making an altar. [Day 18 of 180]

Noah was a remarkable man, showing his faith in so many unwavering ways. If you haven't read his story in a while, it's in Genesis chapters 6–9. During the time of Noah, the world was very wicked, and "every inclination of the thoughts of the human heart was only evil all the time" (Genesis 6:5). Noah was a righteous man, meaning he believed in God. God came to Noah and told him to build an ark, for God was going to destroy the earth and the wicked people but spare Noah and his family. It probably took years for Noah to build the ark, under much scrutiny and ridicule from others. Noah probably waited years for the rain to start. Then he waited months for the floodwaters to dry up. He waited for the dove to return with the olive branch that indicated the presence of dry land. Waiting. Waiting. Waiting. Including waiting on a smelly ark with tons of noisy animals. Has anyone thought about how loud it must have been? Not to mention staying on an ark with only family (no friends) and in likely close quarters. Noah made a lot of sacrifices, and we never hear of him complaining or questioning God once. I imagine myself complaining about how all I want is a latte and a piece of my favorite dark chocolate. I'd complain about how terribly smelly the pigs and skunks are and what I would give for silence! Between the lions roaring and the dogs barking, how would I be able to hear myself think?

The first thing Noah does after he, his family, and all the animals exit the ark is thank God. "Then Noah built an altar to the LORD and, taking some of all the clean animals and clean birds, he sacrificed burnt offerings on it" (Genesis 8:20). Noah had much to be thankful for. He and his family were safe, and God had not given up on the human race or the promise of the Savior. If I were in Noah's shoes, I'd probably do something more self-serving like take a bath or throw a barbeque. As I said in my journal entry, I think my first inkling would be far from building an altar, slaughtering an animal, and praising God.

Burnt offerings and slaughtering animals may sound foreign to you. It sounds strange to me too. But this was the practice for the Old Testament people who believed in God and were looking forward to Jesus' coming to be the ultimate sacrifice. Animal sacrifices were a physical reminder that blood is required to forgive sins, and they foreshadowed the sacrificial work Jesus would accomplish on the cross.

I can only imagine the isolation Noah and his family experienced, how lonely and disheartening it must have been. Everything was destroyed: all people, all buildings, and all establishments. They literally had to start from scratch building, cultivating, and breeding. I feel like Noah and his family might have felt quite a bit of pressure to press the restart button on civilization.

Lord, help me be more like Noah. I want to thank you first, not last. I want to find positivity among an array of perceived negativity. I want my thankfulness to keep me from focusing on what I'm waiting on you to give me. Help me, Lord. Amen.

Change

The day we've been waiting for is here. We closed on our new home! After signing dozens of papers, we got the keys and drove straight to our new house! I don't think it's really hit me quite yet, but I'm feeling extremely thankful. I can't wait to move in and to make our new house a home. [Day 66 of 180]

Last night in Tosa. So bittersweet. It's where we had our first fights as a married couple. It's where we laughed, we cried, and laughed until we cried. [Day 73 of 180]

Change. I wouldn't say that I'm one who loves change. Change is scary and unknown. To move from the comfort of the Milwaukee area was a big change for me. Even though the new house was only about 25 minutes north of the city, it felt like Ben and I were moving away from everything. Moving away from my favorite coffee shop that I'd frequent with my sister-in-law, niece, and nephew. Moving away from walks in the Menomonee River Parkway with Ben. Moving away from the Beer Garden, within walking distance, that Ben and I enjoyed going to with my sister and brother-in-law. Moving away from biking to the Tosa Farmers Market on Saturdays. Moving away from Café Hollander dates with friends and neighbors. It was our first place together: where we had our first fights as a couple; where we navigated being newly-weds together; where we hosted ribfest, many Ultimate Frisbee events, and plenty of friend and family gatherings. The duplex we lived in had tons of character. It was an older home with finishes such as hardwood floors, plaster walls, crown molding, and built-in china cabinets in the dining room. It also had its quirks, but I will miss that home. It isn't just the bones of the house that I miss. It's the countless memories that were made there.

I think what made moving even more monumental was that many other family members were moving around the same time Ben and I were. We weren't the only ones changing while everything else was static, but, rather, we were moving while everything else was in motion. More change in our family. Within three months of Ben and me moving, my aunt officially retired and moved down to Florida with her husband. My other aunt and her two daughters moved out of their house and into a duplex. Then my grandma moved from her independent living apartment to a memory care facility. So many changes, and each move had its own circumstances and trials behind it. It was comforting to remember that Jesus is "the same yesterday and today and forever" (Hebrews 13:8). We don't know what the future holds, but we sure know who holds the future. (I know it's a cliché saying, but it rang true to me in this season of life.)

I had to be reminded that sometimes life needs to get messy before it becomes beautiful again. And sometimes in that mess we find God's grace. I easily got stressed out by the dozens of boxes and bins that needed to be filled up, loaded on the truck, and unpacked (and we didn't even have any kids to pack for yet!). But Ben and I were packing and unpacking for a reason: We were able to afford a new house that had everything on our need list *and* many things on our want list as well. While we know the grass isn't always greener on the other side, we were excited to have more space and a large yard to spread out in and enjoy God's creation.

Sometimes I think it would be better if we could just hurry up and skip through the hard stuff in life, skip through the waves of changes. But I was discovering through my 180 that it is through the bumps and cracks in the road that we see God's grace and redemption. We are reminded that we are not able to maneuver through this life alone without falling flat on our faces.

When I started to feel bogged down by the ever-growing moving to-do lists and tasks, I turned on some Christian music. Immediately I felt my whole attitude change. How can you not become fired up listening to songs that present the gospel with beauty, power, and emotion?

Whatever worry I had previously melted away. God was speaking to me. Instead of focusing on the stress and mess, I was reminded of what I should be thankful for. Thankful Ben and I had so many earthly things to pack up. Thankful we had friends and family to help us move. Thankful for our new home and the new tenants taking over our duplex. Thankful for our jobs to pay for our daily needs and our wants, even though we are undeserving of both.

TRAVEL TIPS: Bible Reading Plan

If I had to do it all over again, I think I would lay out my Bible study plan (one Bible study per week) for the full 180 days *before* beginning my journey. I did not do this and would scramble each week to find a Bible study related to waiting on God more. I think having a Bible study outline ahead of time would shift my focus from "What should I study this week?" to "Wow, look at how much I learned from my Bible study this week!" The Bible sections I ended up using were often inspired by my daily Bible reading with Ben, sermons at church, and my small group Bible study. I also would use the search engine on biblegateway.com to search "waiting on God."

Canoeing

We got back tonight from canoeing the Wisconsin River with Kristen and Ryan. . . . It had rained a ton before we arrived— the river was 3 feet higher than usual. [Day 70 of 180]

Every summer for the last three years we have gone on an overnight canoe trip down the Wisconsin River with two of our dear friends. There's just something about getting away from everyday life. You hear only the river rushing and the birds chirping. The only civilization you see is a rare car driving by on a country highway in the distance. You feel the warm sun on your face and a cool breeze off the river. It's wonderful.

This canoe trip requires a lot of preparation, a lot of which Ben does because he simply enjoys that kind of thing. He loves planning the details, from the route to the times of departure and arrival. He plans the meals, and I don't think I've ever eaten a brat or hot dog on this trip. We've never even had a s'more. Instead of the cliché camping foods, we and our friends have had marinated chicken, sautéed zucchini, or grilled pork for dinner. For lunch we've feasted on gourmet turkey sandwiches complete with pretzel buns. And for breakfast we've eaten omelets stuffed with veggies or fried eggs over shredded, crispy pork. Packing compactly is important, and Ben spends extra time engineering how everything will fit, especially so we can eat well on the river. He's dedicated too. One year he grilled fantastic chicken and corn over the fire in the pouring rain while the rest of us stayed dry inside our tent that we had set up right in the nick of time. He loved it, and so did we!

Every year we have done similar routes on the river, but each time is so different. Different weather, different food, different memories, and different time of the year visited. We always sleep on a different "island" or sandbar every year as well. It's always fun to try and recognize the ones we stayed on in previous years as we paddle leisurely along the river. We reminisce of an amazing sunset on one island and pouring rain on another. We remember the shape of a sandbar and the quirky trees surrounding it.

Yes, every year is unique, but there is one thing that is always the same year after year: the feeling of renewal. I am blessed with rest—a physical and mental break from the stressors of everyday life. Even though I come home with mosquito bites, greasy hair, sore muscles, and sunburns, it's still restful and the river is tranquil. It's always great fellowship too, receiving love and support from our amazing friends and from Ben.

Then there are the mishaps. One year the river was 3 feet higher than normal, and there were no sandbars to sleep on at night. We had to tightrope up into a mosquito-infested island and tie our canoe to a sturdy tree so it wouldn't float away. Another year we (stupidly) didn't reapply sunscreen and our skin became as red as tomatoes. Another year Ben's paddle broke as he was paddling, and the broken wooden piece smashed him in the face. God was watching over Ben that day, protecting him from injuring his eye. Ben happened to be wearing his sunglasses right then. So when the half dry-rotted paddle decided to snap, the sunglasses took the brunt of the impact. They were destroyed, cracked in two, but Ben only got a scrape on his forehead. His eye was uninjured.

These canoe trips are like life in general. There are always bumps, detours, and delays along the way, but that is what makes the adventure sweet. Through life's messy adventures, God shows us himself and his grace even when we aren't waiting on him. Before my 180, I know for a fact that I did not take frequent notice of God's grace, or if I did it would be a fleeting thought only lasting a few seconds. By the end of my 180, I was seeing God's grace more and more in my daily living. I see his grace in my coworkers who notice I'm having a bad day and go above and beyond to help me in any way they can. I see his grace in my patients who show quiet perseverance in the face of death. I see his grace in our vacations, as he keeps us safe from many dangers and provides us with rest. I see his grace in the quiet of the river. I'm still learning, but what I've learned is to slow down and notice God's sweet, unexpected, and sometimes subtle grace.

YOUR TURN

- Have you taken notice of God's grace today? What did you notice?

- What are ways in which you can remind yourself to notice God's grace more?

Patients

I often see the worst of people in my job at the hospital. I see them when they have a fever of 102.4 degrees and have saturated their gown, sheets, and blanket because of their sweat. I see them when they're "loopy" coming off pain medications and sedatives after a procedure. I see grown men cry because they're in so much pain. I see patients after they get the news of "I'm sorry, there's nothing more we can do for your cancer." In a strange way, I feel blessed to be a part of their story. I feel blessed because I can offer a hand to hold, a listening ear, or a wall to vent at. I can be any of those things. The interesting thing is there is never much shame with my patients. They already feel vulnerable in their exposed gown and bright yellow, grippy fall-prevention socks. Why not wear your heart on your sleeve when you already don't feel like yourself?

I honestly feel honored to be a part of these veterans' journeys. The job of being a nurse is exhausting, both physically and emotionally. There are days when I get home and feel like I can't do anything because I'm just drained. I've given my all the entire day to my patients, and when I get home, I don't have much to give to Ben. It's a sacrifice, but as hard and busy as some days can be, I have never once thought about quitting. I did eventually figure out I needed to cut down my hours some, and that decision helped me keep a better work-life balance.

People often say, "You are helping these patients so much," but often I feel like the opposite is true. I learn so much from my patients.

I learn from the patients who have family who visit them. I see how much the families care for their loved ones who are hospitalized. One family stays all night to help comfort their loved one. Another family drives two hours to visit every evening and then drives two hours home again before rising early the next morning for work. I see how important family is for a patient's healing. I am filled with deep thankfulness that neither I nor any of my family members are in a hospital bed.

I also learn from the patients who don't have family or whose families don't visit them. Many of these patients somehow maintain a positive attitude and outlook despite not having a hand to hold. God is more faithful even than family, more faithful than anyone.

At the beginning of the book of Proverbs, there's a long list of promises to tell us just how wise these proverbs can make us. I truly feel like my patients are not just my calling: they are my proverbs. I am thankful for how God works in my life through them:

> for gaining wisdom and instruction;
> for understanding words of insight;
> for receiving instruction in prudent behavior,
> doing what is right and just and fair;
> for giving prudence to those who are simple,
> knowledge and discretion to the young.
> (Proverbs 1:2-4)

I really do learn something new at my job every day, and not just about labs, tests, or disease processes. I learn better how to cope, how to love, and how to listen. I learn how I want to advocate for my own child and my other family members. I have learned that even on the hardest, most patience-trying day, I come home healthy to my loving, healthy husband and child and a house I adore, and most important, every day and night I know that my Jesus is King.

Rachel

*Today we enjoyed our last day in Door County. This trip defi-
nitely made me once again appreciate the wonderful friends in
my life. Today, Rachel and I had a long heart-to-heart on the
dock. She talked to me more about her adoptive mom than ever
before. [Day 56 of 180]*

I met my dear friend Rachel in 2009 at Camp Phillip, a Christian summer
camp in central Wisconsin where we worked together. We served as camp
counselors there throughout our summers in college. From the day we
met, we immediately clicked as friends. Not only do we have the same
passions (Jesus, family, camp, friends), but we also have complementary
personalities that seem to draw out the best in each of us.

Rachel was adopted from Colombia when she was six months old.
Her older brother was also adopted from South Korea. After Rachel married her childhood sweetheart in the summer of 2013, her father gave
her a box of keepsakes he'd been saving at his house. As she was sorting
through the box one day, she discovered her hospital birth records that
gave her biological mother's full name. Rachel had never seen this docu-
ment before! She had always known her birth mother's first and last name
but never her middle name. That same evening, her curiosity got to her,
and she decided to search her birth mom's full name on Facebook. She
found what appeared to be her birth mom's profile, and scrolling through
the pictures she saw a young woman who looked exactly like her. "What
if that's my sister?" she wondered. In all her years in the US, she had never
seen anyone who looked like her.

I remember Rachel calling Ben and me that night, believing she had
found her mom on Facebook and weighing the pros and cons of what
to do. Thoughts were racing through her head: "Should I message her?
What if she doesn't want to be in contact with me? What if she's not my
mom?" Ben and I saw the picture of the woman Rachel presumed to be
her sister, and she really did look identical to Rachel. Trying to be calm,
we told her to think and pray about the situation and sleep on it. There
was no reason to decide that night. Rachel did just that, and she only

became more convinced that she should reach out to this woman. She messaged this person, her assumed birth mom, and then she waited. And waited. No response.

Nine months passed.

Rachel thought it was a lost cause and that it had been too good to be true. But then she noticed that the friend request she had sent this woman had disappeared from her Facebook page. It normally said "pending." She decided to give it one more chance. She would send this person, possibly her birth mom, one last friend request. This time the woman saw the friend request, and when Rachel came home that night, she had a little red number 1 in her message box. It was her birth mom!

As it turns out, Rachel has a sister who is two years older than she, and a half brother in high school. Rachel always knew from her adoptive parents that she had a biological mom and sister in Colombia, but she never knew about a half brother. Rachel thought this was perfect; she had always wanted a little brother!

Thankfully, communicating with her biological family was possible because Rachel spoke Spanish. It had long been Rachel's dream to find and thank her birth mom for putting her up for adoption and tell her that she grew up to be a happy, healthy Christian woman. This dream is what drove Rachel to learn Spanish, so that if she ever went back to Colombia, she could speak her native language. She even studied abroad in Spain for a semester to become more fluent, and she has a second major in Spanish. She quickly formed a relationship with her overseas family through social media apps: texting, sharing pictures, and video chatting.

In January 2016, Rachel traveled to her birthplace of Bogota, Colombia, for four weeks to meet her biological family for the first time. Her husband and her adoptive dad accompanied her. It was the most epic trip of a lifetime!

Rachel's stomach was twisting and turning all the way there. She had always been curious where she could have grown up or with whom, but she had always found peace knowing that God had planned her unique adoptive family. Now there was another family. She wondered how she would fit in and if her Spanish was up to par to translate for her dad and her husband. She read Spanish books most of the plane ride there, but after a while she realized that if she didn't know something in Spanish by then, there was no use in trying to learn it now. She was feeling nervous about interacting with her biological family members. She did not want to disappoint them! What if they had different expectations of her, a different definition of how family should act? Through video chat, she had already learned she giggled like them, rolled her eyes like them, and blushed like them. It had never occurred to her that her birth family must have matching faces. But now meeting in person was so much more intimate.

Rachel felt deep uncertainty. The thought of responding to the words *daughter* and *sister* was surreal to her. It was almost the same feeling she had shortly after she married her husband and was asked to call her mother-in-law "Mom." At that time, she hadn't used that name for nine years, since her adoptive mom had passed away. Her husband's encouragement helped her to be brave, embrace the change, and ease into it.

Now this was even more intense. Rachel knew that the moment she embraced her birth mom and called her Mamá, they both would be filled with emotions, not just of love but also of grief—grief they had set aside for years. Rachel's birth mother had lost her own mom when she was 19. Rachel had lost her adoptive mom when she was 13. Through Christ, they each had found contentment over the years knowing their mothers were in heaven. For Rachel, hugging her Mamá would mean having a mother-daughter relationship, one which her birth mother had never dreamed of. Rachel's birth mom had kept her pregnancy hidden from her family. When she was giving birth, the medical team held a sheet in front of her eyes so that she couldn't change her mind about giving Rachel up for adoption. She only heard Rachel's first cry and never even saw her face.

When Rachel stepped off the plane, she looked around everywhere: out the windows at the Andes Mountains of Bogota, at the many Colombian faces around her, and at her family's American faces. She instantly began translating signs and navigating her husband and her father through customs. She told the customs officer about her story, meeting her biological family, and returning to her orphanage, and he warmly welcomed her.

Rachel's dad wanted to stop at a gift shop prior to meeting her biological family. At the checkout, Rachel glanced at the baggage claim and noticed a wall of large glass windows. For the first time, she saw her birth mom from far away, and her mom saw her too. Rachel's heart started pounding. She could tell from far away that her mom was tearing up. Rachel looked at her husband and said she needed to use the restroom because she was feeling nauseated and hot. She splashed cold water on her face, trying to call it a normal day.

Rachel returned to her dad and husband, who already had gathered their bags, and they began to walk outside to the other side of the glass. The moment she was outside with her new family, her heart exploded! Her mom's loving arms were so welcoming. Her sister had a calm spirit, and her brother's smile gave Rachel peace. Rachel watched her biological family embrace her husband and her dad, and she was thankful both families were able to meet one another. Just like that, they had broken the ice and were all one family. Rachel had been prepared to meet four people, but to her surprise a ton of extended family came to the airport too: a grandma on her biological dad's side, cousins, and even the family bulldog!

During the trip, their group visited the orphanage where Rachel had once lived. It was very nostalgic for her dad. One of his favorite stories to tell for years now is about when he and Rachel's adoptive mom went to Columbia and met the orphanage founder. This trip, however, the orphanage was in a different building. Back in 1991, the orphanage was raising money to relocate to a new building. Now in 2016, it was very special for her dad to see the result of his and many others' donations. Since the founder had passed away, their group met one of the founder's daughters and got to share with her the story of Rachel's reunion with her birth mom.

Touring the orphanage gave Rachel insight into how blessed she was to have been adopted. She learned that her birth mom was only about three months pregnant when she had decided to give Rachel up for adoption. At the time, she was grieving her husband's death. Her husband had been killed in a bombing caused by the drug cartel, leaving her with no source of income and a toddler (Rachel's older sister) to take care of. Many of the children at the orphanage are ineligible for adoption because, interestingly enough, many of them are not true orphans. Most of the children there have at least one living parent or family member who loves and wants them but feels like he or she doesn't have the proper resources to care for them. By law, these children cannot be adopted unless their parents terminate their parental rights, so many children are stuck there until they are 18 years old. One worker at the orphanage in Columbia told Rachel that many parents cannot stand the idea that their child will have another mom or dad and this selfishness is the reason many children are left there. Rachel had a new appreciation for her birth mom, realizing how brave and selfless she had been to give her up for adoption. Rachel and her husband have plans to adopt a child as well someday.

One night after staying up late spending time with family, Rachel's dad was headed off to bed and met Rachel's birth mom in the hallway. She had to ask him a question. Of course, that meant Rachel had to translate even at this late hour.

Her birth mom asked him, "Can you tell me about your wife, Rachel's mom? I want to know her."

With tears welling up in his eyes and his hand over his heart, Rachel's dad replied, "She was a loving mother and adored her children. She was kind and happy, and the moment she held Rachel it was love. I have a special picture of me holding her at the orphanage for the first time."

The rest of the conversation went like this:

"I never got to hold her, even see her. They covered my eyes after she was born. I always wondered about her. I'm so sorry you lost your wife. She sounds like she was the best mom for Rachel. But you have such a big heart, I can tell. You loved my daughter. You were such a good father to her."

"I love her, but my wife was so full of love."

Rachel chimed in, "My dad was always there for us."

Then her birth mom said, "I love your wife and you so much for caring for Rachel all these years. I'm so happy that you were her parents. You have been so strong for her."

"No, I just try my best with God's help. We always told her about you and how we were so thankful for you giving us your daughter. We always promised to bring her back to Colombia."

"Yes, thanks be to God. Only he knows best, and I'm glad you came back."

"Yes, exactly, God always had a plan."

Rachel spent most of the conversation holding back tears of joy and awe while stumbling through this emotional translation. Her heart was bursting from both the joy and the sorrow her parents had felt all those years. She felt unbelievably blessed to have witnessed this conversation, and even though life had been messy and imperfect, she knew this was exactly what God wanted for her. God wanted Rachel and her dad to meet her biological family and have the opportunity to thank her birth mom for loving her enough to give her up for adoption. God blessed all three of them that night with gratitude and contentment.

Through this experience, Rachel's faith in God has grown. God has given her the gift of knowing that her biological family members are Christian. Otherwise, she would always have wondered. It has given her great comfort knowing they share the same faith in Jesus.

Rachel has been humbled by this experience too. She wonders how she got so lucky. God tells us that in all things he "works for the good of those who love him" (Romans 8:28). When we see him working for our good in such dramatic ways, it moves us to love him all the more. Rachel feels so grateful now for God's plan and for a whole new family to love and serve.

Rachel's story has inspired those around her. Her birth mom's selfless trust, her adoptive parents' dedicated love, her Savior's gifts of Baptism and faith—all of these encourage those who know Rachel to continue to love new people in their lives and take every opportunity to show Christ's love.

Rachel never thought that her dream of meeting her biological mom would come true. Through God's perfect timing, Rachel met her Mamá at the perfect time. Her birth mom and half brother even flew out to Wisconsin for Rachel's graduation for her master's degree in occupational therapy. Rachel never could have predicted that her adoptive mom would pass away from cancer at an early age, but she also couldn't have predicted the amount of love poured out to her from her biological family. God is there through the mountains and valleys, and thankfully he's there to see us through to the end.

Rachel has been an inspiration to me for years but even more so during my 180. God let the two of us spend some vacation time together up in Door County. In answer to my prayers to him to show me people who are good at waiting on him, he gave me a couple of hours to sit with Rachel on a dock overlooking Clark Lake, and she told me like never before about her whole lifetime of waiting. Waiting on God to show her why she had to be adopted. To show her he knew her heart's desire to be hugged by her birth mom someday. Rachel didn't even know I was writing a book about waiting on God. Yes, Rachel has taught me how to be resilient through some tough times of waiting and how to be thankful when the waiting ends in showers of blessings. But she has also taught me how to be thankful *before* the waiting ends. All those years of never knowing what her biological family members were like or if she would ever meet them, Rachel had trusted God, grateful for the life he had given her. Living not in what-ifs or resenting God but loving him for the adoptive family who love her so much.

YOUR TURN

- Is there someone in your life you admire who has exemplified waiting on God more? Or whatever 180 journal topic you may choose: loving God more, etc.

- Have you ever told someone that you look up to them when it comes to serving God?

- When you're in a tough situation, how do you focus your time and energy waiting on God? Has there been a time in your life when God took a tough situation and turned it into a huge blessing you did not expect?

Stories

Throughout my 180 journey, specific people in my life showed me in dramatic ways what "waiting on God" really looked like.

Most people would call it "luck" that my friends and family depicted what "waiting on God" looked like at the exact same time I was studying the topic. I wouldn't call it luck; I'd call it grace. God purposefully placed these people in my life to teach me a lesson. I was praying he would help me notice them, and he did. It wasn't just to teach them and me a lesson but to help others as well. I'm certain the people I talk about in this book are shining examples to those around them of God's grace and what it means to have strength in Jesus even when it's hard to keep waiting. I want to share their stories with you because they have taught me what it means to wait on God. None of them knew I was working on this project at the time God was working through them, but I shared with them after the fact how much I learned through observing them.

These "stories" happen all the time in everyday life, but sometimes we don't stop to ponder what God has taught others or taught us or the significance of such lessons and life events. That is where journaling became imperative. Journaling forced me to stop, ponder, wonder, question, pray, and think. I could safely put my confused thoughts in ink on paper and sort through what God wanted me to learn. Nothing in this life is random; God has a plan for you. I would encourage you to pray for God to bring forward people in your life as great examples to learn from during your 180 journey.

TRAVEL TIPS: Your Stories

I don't know about you, but I learn best from experience and other people's stories. When I was studying in nursing school, I would often try to connect a concept with a patient I had cared for in a clinical. I would try to come up with a story, song, or picture to help me remember the details in challenging subjects like pathophysiology and pharmacology. That's just how my brain works.

Such is true in my spiritual life as well. I tend to remember a biblical truth from a sermon when the pastor connects it to a story that hits home for me or uses it to provide insight for a compelling real-life situation. I can remember this story or situation days, weeks, months, and even years later. From remembering the stories, I can experience again the lesson I learned that day.

For my 180 journey, I learned best by watching and listening with an ear bent on learning and gleaning from those around me, those God placed in my life to teach me what waiting on God more meant. I also prayed daily that God would help me notice people in my life who were waiting on him. Here are a few tips for your journey to help you recognize and cherish those stories right in front of you:

↻ Pray that God places people in your life who exemplify what you are focused on during your journey.

↻ Pray that God helps you notice people in your life who exemplify what you are focused on during your journey.

↻ Reread your journal entries under a new lens of your topic to help you see a new perspective you didn't notice before.

↻ Throughout your day, pause to think and pray about your topic in connection with the days' events to see if God is perhaps trying to teach you something on your topic.

↻ Talk to your accountability partner, your friends, and your family about your topic and see if they have any examples that may help you.

Happiness vs. Joy

There is a debate about happiness and joy and what the Bible says about them. Are they the same? Are they different?

Some say they are very different. Happiness is just an emotion. It's fleeting; it's external. It's based on people, experiences, events, and surroundings—it's based on things that change, how life happens to be treating us at a given moment. But joy is a way of being, a state of mind, a mindset. The Bible actually urges us to be joyful even in difficult situations: "Rejoice in the Lord always. I will say it again: Rejoice!" (Philippians 4:4). "Consider it pure joy, my brothers and sisters, whenever you face trials of many kinds" (James 1:2). "Rejoice always" (1 Thessalonians 5:16). Joy is constant, not dependent on the happenings in everyday life.

Others do not believe there is a difference between joy and happiness: they are one and the same.

My takeaway from this debate is that joy is an internal peace. Sometimes as Christians we confuse God with a genie. We want things of this world to immediately make us happy. We want answers to our prayers to come as if at the touch of a button. But we have, in our certainty that Jesus loves us, an internal joy not influenced by the world. It is a gladness of heart dependent only on our Savior, on his forgiveness, on his resurrection, on all the ways he sets us free. It is an unchanging demeanor because it comes from knowing God's unchanging grace, the unfailing generosity of his heart.

Sometimes I wait on God to give me nicer feelings. What I often forget is that I am completely undeserving of joy or happiness. The fact that I can even pray to God about my feelings or anything else—and that I can confidently expect his answer—is completely and utterly amazing. The fact that God's feelings toward me never turn sour, no matter how impatient I become—that's amazing too. All this we call grace, God's undeserved generous love. The feelings will come. Grace I have right now. Happiness will come. Joy I have right now!

Waiting on God Means Hanging on to Hope in Situations That May Not Be Resolved in This Life

Is Worry Firing?

Awesome sermon today from Pastor Bondow based on the "Do not worry" section in Luke, which just so happens to be one of my favorites. Pastor Bondow said today, "If worry is firing, something spiritually is not firing." I just think this is a great image for me, being one who tends to worry. Worrying means a lack of trust in God. I was worried about getting 5K sponsors, and now this year we have a record of seven. [Day 43 of 180]

Not only did Rachel and I meet at camp, but I met my husband, Ben, at camp as well. Ben and I stopped working at Camp Phillip right before graduating from college so that we could begin our careers. Even though we did not work there anymore, we still found ways to serve despite not physically being there. Ben used his talents as a structural engineer, donating his time to design a new cabin/conference center. Together we orchestrated the Camp Phillip 5K fundraiser for several years. Our canoe adventure friend was the one who started the first Camp Phillip 5K, which was an enormous success, and Ben and I took it over. It's a lot of work, but it's a fun and active way to support Camp Phillip. All the proceeds directly support the camp, since the business sponsors cover the cost of the supplies, food, banners, and T-shirts.

Ben and I were planning the 5K as I was journaling. I was worried we wouldn't get enough sponsors. But God blessed us above and beyond and gave us seven sponsors, our largest number of sponsors yet! We were also worried to see only 70 participants preregistered for the race. The year previous we had 100 participants, and our goal was to have 120 that year. Guess what? God blessed us with a little over 120 participants, with an overwhelming number of same-day sign-ups. Over and over again, I see that God is in control. Why even waste my time worrying?

But I'm impatient. I wanted to have 120 participants preregistered before we arrived. I wanted the sponsors committed months earlier. I wrote about this worry in my journal. I wanted it to be easy, stress-free even, but instead God showed me his timing. He showed me his grace. He showed me his power. This is just one way God has had me wait in life, and he leads me closer to him time and time again.

God wants his children to step out in faith when relying on him. When I was a camp counselor working those blissful summers in central Wisconsin (they really were!), each cabin had its own Bible study as one of the daily activities for the campers. I truly enjoyed this time with my campers, listening and learning from them. My favorite memory of a cabin Bible study is one about Joshua. Joshua had been the right-hand man of Moses, leading the people of Israel out of their cruel slavery in Egypt. After Moses' death, Joshua led the Israelites, some two million of them, of all ages, through the wilderness. God promised them a new land to live in, "a land flowing with milk and honey" (Exodus 3:8). But between them and this new land stood the Jordan River, running quickly due to the snowmelt from the mountains in the north. I can just imagine what that looked like after that one canoe trip when the Wisconsin River was at flood stage. I can't imagine swimming across that, much less trying to get a family across it with all the household goods (and farm animals too). God gave Joshua the instructions that when the Israelites came upon the Jordan River, the priests who carried the ark of the covenant were to go first. The ark was a huge golden chest with golden angels on top of it in which God had promised his presence would always be. The priests were to go ahead of the people and stand in the water. Then all the water in the river would be stopped. I can imagine the priests were very careful of their footing: river rocks can be slippery, and it would be terrible if the priests accidentally dropped the ark into the river. Not until all their toes touched the water, only then, did the water upstream stop flowing, "piled up in a heap a great distance away" (Joshua 3:16). All those families with their belongings, herds, and flocks crossed into their new land on completely dry ground. This story was always a great visual reminder to me: Christians need to be willing to jump feetfirst into the Jordan River. We can trust in God's promises even if the rocks are slippery and the water is high.

I wanted to see the fruits of my labor at the 5K. I wanted to see proof on paper before the weekend began that it was going to be successful with a record number of sponsors and a record number of participants. But God taught me a valuable lesson. He wanted me to put my feet in the water. The Israelites would have been thankful either way, whether the river was stopped before or after the priests put their feet in the river. The priests stepping into the water first, however, showed the people what stepping out in faith and trusting in God looked like. They saw that he would stay true to his promises. Some people like to know the ending of a book or movie before they begin. It's the unknown, the suspense, that scares them. But that's what waiting on God is all about. It's about depending on and trusting in the Savior to keep his children safe, provide what they need, and pour out his blessings.

It isn't just the small things in life. God says we don't have to worry even when we don't know where the next day's meal money is going to come from or where our family will sleep tomorrow night. God reminds us in his Word not to worry:

> I tell you, do not worry about your life, what you
> will eat or drink; or about your body, what you will
> wear. Is not life more than food, and the body more
> than clothes? Look at the birds of the air; they do not
> sow or reap or store away in barns, and yet your heav-
> enly Father feeds them. Are you not much more valu-
> able than they? Can any one of you by worrying add a

single hour to your life? And why do you worry about clothes? See how the flowers of the field grow. They do not labor or spin. Yet I tell you that not even Solomon in all his splendor was dressed like one of these. If that is how God clothes the grass of the field, which is here today and tomorrow is thrown into the fire, will he not much more clothe you—you of little faith? So do not worry, saying, "What shall we eat?" or "What shall we drink?" or "What shall we wear?" For the pagans run after all these things, and your heavenly Father knows that you need them. But seek first his kingdom and his righteousness, and all these things will be given to you as well. Therefore do not worry about tomorrow, for tomorrow will worry about itself. Each day has enough trouble of its own. (Matthew 6:25-34)

The sentence "Do not worry about tomorrow, for tomorrow will worry about itself" should be plastered everywhere in my home, in my car, and at work. I need this reminder more than daily. I need it constantly. God says that the pagans concentrate on food, drink, and clothes. Why? Because they do not know or trust in the Savior. Because the things God wants them to concentrate on don't really matter to them.

Everyday life has worries. I was worried about the success of the 5K. God once again showed me what a waste of time worrying is. How wasteful it was to overly focus on it and lose sleep over it. God does not want his people to worry, but, rather, he wants us to go to him in prayer. "Do not be anxious about anything, but in every situation, by prayer and petition, with thanksgiving, present your requests to God" (Philippians 4:6). During this time, God worked through Ben encouraging me not to worry and to focus on God and his promises.

But even when the worries get bigger than the everyday variety, God says to wait on him instead. I have never known the kind of poverty where one has to ask, "What will we eat? How will we survive the winter?" I know that if I am ever in that much need, God will take care of me. He will give me what I need for what is most important: my eternal life.

YOUR TURN

- What kind of worry is firing in your life right now?
- How can you turn the worry over to God, to wait on him more?
- What are some ways you can remind yourself in everyday life not to worry but to turn worry over to God?

Me Before You

*This is life without God—not waiting on God to show your
"usefulness" to society: there's no hope. [Day 118 of 180]*

I was looking forward to seeing a movie called *Me Before You*. I guess the
title of the film should have been a red flag, but I had high expectations
based on the previews I had seen.

The film takes place in England and follows the life of Lou, a young
woman from a family of modest means, who becomes a caregiver for a
wealthy young man named Will. Will sustained injuries a couple years
prior that left him a quadriplegic, unable to use any of his limbs. The
previews depicted an endearing story of love and positive change.

What you don't expect from the previews is that Will, overwhelmed
by his affliction, had made plans to travel to Switzerland and have himself
euthanized. You find out in the film that upon meeting Lou, he already
had made these final plans. His sorrow was too great. Mourning the loss
of his mobility, his utility, and his dignity, he yearned for his pre-accident
life. The film made me question how I would feel if I were Will in this
situation. There is an underlying sadness to the story. Will doesn't have
any faith to rely on. As the movie progresses, he seems to put his faith,
trust, and friendship in Lou.

After hearing Will's plan and troubled by his decision, Will's parents
request that he live at home for six months before going through with
his decision. Their hope is that he will be surrounded by their love and
rethink ending his life. Then enters Lou. She is initially in the dark about
Will's plans. At the start, Will wants nothing to do with her joyful attitude
and cheery demeanor. His actions range from terse to all-out rude to
Lou. It made me angry watching him treat Lou, this beautiful source of
joy, with such disdain. The film encouraged me to see the world through
Will's perspective. I can understand why he felt bitter and sorrowful. He
lost his independence, his friends, and his job. I found myself rooting for
Lou to break through to Will.

Just when Lou is beginning to soften Will and have feelings for him,
she becomes aware of his decision. She is devastated, feeling betrayed that

he would choose death over her. She decides that she will do everything within her power to change his mind. A slow transformation occurs. Lou cheerfully persists in trying to make him smile, and eventually she succeeds. She encourages him to get out of the house, and eventually he allows her to take him on outings, including horse races and even on a date to a wedding.

It appears that Lou is swaying Will's mind, and they begin to fall in love with each other. She's convinced that she has succeeded, that he has given up his plans of assisted suicide and will choose life. But at the end of the six months (spoiler alert), Will ultimately decides to go to Switzerland to die. The movie portrays it as a selfless decision, that Will is letting Lou live her life to the fullest. He says he doesn't want to hold her back, even though she's told him that he wouldn't. She tells Will, "I know we can do this. I know it's not how you would have chosen it, but I know I can make you happy. And all I can say is that you make me . . . you make me into someone I couldn't even imagine. You make me happy, even when you're awful, I would rather be with you—even the you that you seem to think is diminished—than with anyone else in the world." This movie ended so sourly in my opinion. It tried to make euthanasia look pretty and peaceful, having it happen in a beautiful, white, and airy Switzerland home with Lou and Will's parents by his side. Lou loved Will, and he loved her. But ultimately he decides that what is best for himself is leaving Lou and his parents broken.

I finished the film with a pit in my stomach. In the hour and a half of the movie, I connected with Will and Lou. I experienced Will's heart soften. I watched the loving determination of Lou. I saw Lou fight for her loved one. I just wanted Will to choose life.

While I journaled after watching this film, I found that I was angry with Will. I thought him selfish. While writing and processing what I saw, I realized that I struggled to really put myself in his shoes. Yes, the movie did a great job conveying his sorrow, his frustration, and his desire to escape his troubles, but I found that I really didn't understand his decision. What would drive someone to decide to end his own life? It hit me how blessed I am in two ways: I have never been in a situation this difficult, and I will never be in a situation where my Savior is not there to help me.

I felt like Will was selfish, not just ignoring what his loved ones wanted but also ignoring what God wanted. I suppose that is easy for me to say. I have never been a quadriplegic. Perhaps Will would say it was selfish of his parents and Lou to want to deny him a dignified death when his life felt so unbearable. Perhaps Will would even say it was selfish of God to say, "Trust in me, no matter how much I destroy your body." I don't want to make light of how great a temptation it could be to die.

At the same time, God tells us in his Word that he made each and every one of us for a purpose, and this gift of life is meant for us to use. He wants us to use all the abilities he has given us to the fullest: to spread the Word and make more disciples of Jesus. This truth can be hard to believe, can't it? The truth that God created us each individually and we are miraculously made. Psalm 139:13,14 says, "You created my inmost being; you knit me together in my mother's womb. I praise you because I am fearfully and wonderfully made; your works are wonderful, I know that full well." We also know that God has planned each of our lives: " 'For I know the plans I have for you,' declares the LORD, 'plans to prosper you and not to harm you, plans to give you hope and a future'" (Jeremiah 29:11). This truth can be very hard to believe sometimes, can't it? God knows each of us on an in-depth level, even better than a wife knows her husband. He knows what makes us joyful, what worries us, and what makes us who we are. He knows our quirks and insecurities. He knows our future: what mistakes we will make and what successes we will have. We are each valued and loved by God, even if we don't feel that we are loved by anyone else. "Are not five sparrows sold for two pennies? Yet not one of them is forgotten by God. Indeed, the very hairs of your head are all numbered. Don't be afraid; you are worth more than many sparrows" (Luke 12:6,7). Even though in God's Word we hear time and time again how much he loves us, it can still be hard to believe, can't it? With all of the crime, hostility, hate, and lies in the world today, how can there be love? How can God love me? Me, the person who ruined someone's good name at work, who snapped at my husband, and who lost patience with my son?

The devil is sneaky and very convincing. He wants us to be miserable and struggle with proving our usefulness to society, both of which are real for a person who is a quadriplegic (or anyone with a disability). He convinces us that society would be less burdened without us. With the devil in our lives, it's easy to stop waiting on God and instead take things into our own hands. God is all powerful and loving, but he has no reason to fill us in on his plan or his timing. Take comfort in knowing he loves you and has a plan for you. God may not even reveal his will to us in this life.

God wants us to be a light to those around us, even people like Will. Even though Will and Lou are fictional characters, I was led to wonder, "What would it have taken to change Will's mind?" To think that I would have been able to get through to him if I were Lou in this situation is naive. What Will needed most was a Savior. He needed to hear that he was loved, that he could do God's work, and that when God finally called him from this earth, he would spend eternity in heaven with a perfect body. God makes it clear in his Word that he has a plan for each of his children. Paul in the book of Romans says it best:

> I urge you, brothers and sisters, in view of God's mercy, to offer your bodies as a living sacrifice, holy and pleasing to God—this is your true and proper worship. Do not conform to the pattern of this world, but be transformed by the renewing of your mind. Then you will be able to test and approve what God's will is—his good, pleasing and perfect will. For by the grace given me I say to every one of you: Do not think of yourself more highly than you ought, but rather think of yourself with sober judgment, in accordance with the faith God has distributed to each of you. For just as each of us has one body with many members, and these members do not all have the same function, so in Christ we, though many, form one body, and each member belongs to all the others. We have different gifts, according to the grace given to each of us. If your gift is prophesying, then prophesy in accordance with your faith; if it is serving, then serve; if it is teaching, then teach; if it is to encourage, then give encouragement; if it is giving, then

give generously; if it is to lead, do it diligently; if it is to show mercy, do it cheerfully. (Romans 12:1-8)

Make no mistake: this life will have hardships. Yet we have a God who promises to help lessen the load. "Come to me, all you who are weary and burdened, and I will give you rest. Take my yoke upon you and learn from me, for I am gentle and humble in heart, and you will find rest for your souls. For my yoke is easy and my burden is light" (Matthew 11:28-30). He also reminds us of the great fact that Christ has already overcome the world. He has taken away our troubles. "I have told you these things, so that in me you may have peace. In this world you will have trouble. But take heart! I have overcome the world" (John 16:33). This passage gives me so much hope when the world seems too much to bear. We have our Savior who lived a life on this earth without sin and endured death on the cross so we could live. We are bought with the blood of Jesus. Remember God's time is exactly that: God's time. Knowing this truth should give us strength in the waiting because we know that he holds the answers to our questions and is our comfort during trials.

After seeing *Me Before You*, it hit me just how many times I make that phrase the title of my life. God has a plan for my life, just as he has a plan for your life. Yet I continually find myself making selfish decisions instead of placing my trust in my Savior. God has carried me through the hardest times in my life and never once left my side. His timing is perfect even if I don't understand it. Instead of making the title of my life "Me Before You," I need to offer my life as a living sacrifice to him, trust in him, and wait on him. I need to make the title of my life "Him Before Me."

YOUR TURN

- Have you ever felt like Will in the movie? Have you known someone who felt that way? What caused it?

- Euthanasia is becoming more and more prevalent in today's society. Is there anything you can do to encourage people who feel like there is nothing left to live for? What do they most need or most need to hear?

Hope in the Waiting

Last Saturday we had the Briggs & Al's Run/Walk to support Children's Hospital. On the back of the t-shirt, our group had matching artwork that Melissa designed supporting our loved one. The artwork was a large heart with the Milwaukee cityscape carved into it. Instead of it being rectangular buildings, the cityscape resembled a heart rhythm. It was cool to see so many decorated shirts supporting their loved ones, or company shirts supporting Children's Hospital, or the nurses from the cardiac intensive care unit. Thousands of people gathered together for one purpose, but each for a different reason. [Day 76 of 180]

Have you ever been to an event where thousands of people are there, each for specific personal reasons, but still every heart is throbbing toward the same overarching goal? It's truly amazing and powerful. During my 180, I had the opportunity to participate in the Briggs and Al's Run and Walk to support Children's Hospital of Wisconsin. Thousands of people gathered in downtown Milwaukee, each for their own reason. Maybe it was the parent of a child who had received countless chemo treatments, or perhaps it was a nurse from the cardiac ICU who sees God's wonders happen daily in the work of extremely gifted cardiac surgeons. Maybe a grandmother was at the event, a grandmother who had taken on the responsibility of parent and had been made to feel at home at Children's. Each group of people participating had the option to design the backs of their T-shirts for the event. I couldn't help but become emotional seeing the backs of some T-shirts: "In memory of _____ 1992–2000." Everyone has a story, a hard story, but the people are there for one purpose. They want to help the hospital make other families' hard stories a little easier.

This particular Briggs and Al's Run and Walk our family attended in the summer of 2016 felt extra meaningful. Someone dear to us was recovering from surgery at Children's. We walked in her honor.

But it was also meaningful for another reason: my 180. Observing all the families at the event who had come to depend on and feel at home at Children's made me think about how much waiting these families endured. I thought about how many appointments they've waited for, lab results that were sent out and took weeks to come back, and schedules of various specialty appointments, X-rays, and CT scans. I thought about what it must feel like to wait for recovery and pray for positive news from the doctor or to wait and not know how to pray. The list goes on. There is so much waiting. If you haven't gathered yet from this book, I really am not very good at waiting. I find myself constantly trying to play God in certain parts of my life instead of letting him BE God of my entire life.

Then I think of all the people in attendance that day who were walking in memory of someone. Waiting can be difficult, but what must they be feeling? I would bet anything that they would gladly go back to a life of waiting if they could spend just one more day with their child.

While everyone walked for their own reasons, they all walked for someone. Everyone there had a heart for helping children. Everyone there wanted to show their support to children and families struggling with some of the hardest trials of their lives. My heart broke for all the people who must be going through these tough times without the support and love of Jesus.

I cannot imagine life without Jesus as a rock, especially when it comes to sickness, let alone sickness of children. Jesus, the Savior from sin, does not have any bad results. He is constant, and comes through on all his promises. We know this because of what he communicates to us in his Word. He tells us he has already run the race for us. God says, "So do not fear, for I am with you; do not be dismayed, for I am your God. I will strengthen you and help you; I will uphold you with my righteous right hand" (Isaiah 41:10). God also tells us in his Word, "Come to me, all you who are weary and burdened, and I will give you rest" (Matthew 11:28). Jesus, the Savior of the world, loved us so much that he didn't just create the way to heaven, but he also promised to help us on our journey there.

Ultimately, Christ is the Great Physician, and there is no disease, diagnosis, or prognosis too great for him.

When Jesus came into Peter's house, he saw Peter's mother-in-law lying in bed with a fever. He touched her hand and the fever left her, and she got up and began to wait on him. When evening came, many who were demon-possessed were brought to him, and he drove out the spirits with a word and healed all the sick. This was to fulfill what was spoken through the prophet Isaiah: "He took up our infirmities and bore our diseases." (Matthew 8:14-17)

These words from Isaiah and Matthew reveal just how blessed we are to be helped and comforted by Jesus. But what about the times we don't see God's love, support, or plan? What must the people running or walking "in memory" feel? I question God's plan when I struggle with a bad cold. What must they feel to have seen their children endure so much hardship? Why didn't God give them rest? While Christ is the Great Physician, it doesn't mean he takes away all suffering. While Jesus' love is boundless, it doesn't mean that there won't be hardships in this life. We may never know the whys in this life, but God does.

There is hope. There is hope that God has a plan through it all. There is hope that Jesus is with us each step of the way. There is hope that we can be beacons of his light to the world. There is hope that no matter how much believers may suffer, they will find rest in the arms of their Savior.

Being at a large event like the Briggs and Al's Run and Walk had me thinking how much hope was there that day. The people in attendance had seen some of the hardest times. Some, I imagine, were exhausted. Some were mourning. All seemed hopeful. They had hope that through their trials, good could be done. I only wish that all the people there would have hope in their Savior.

I think about what I have waited for in my life. I think back on all the times I thought I knew better than God—that if I did X, he would do Y. Then I think back on the people at this event, whether they were parents or neurosurgeons. There is nothing to do but wait sometimes. That is true in all our lives. We need to wait on God even when it seems impossible—especially when it seems impossible.

YOUR TURN

- Have you noticed others around you going through extra waiting in life? How can you encourage those who are in the trenches of waiting day in and day out?

Valuing Life

Stories like those of Rachel, Amy, Will, and the children for whom people walked that 5K event caused me to think about how valuable life is. All these lives are important to God, and Christians need to think about the sanctity of life at the beginning and end of life.

I thank God that Amy's parents and Rachel's mom chose life over abortion. When I hear of mothers whose doctors push for termination of pregnancy because the child might have Down syndrome or some other issue, I pray that they choose life despite the apparent health challenges. It is always uplifting when families strongly believe that life should be protected and fought for and they use their stories to support the pro-life cause.

There is no denying that the overwhelming majority of people in the world believe that murder is wrong. At their core, people are wired to value their own life and the lives of other people around them. People drive safely to protect their lives and the lives of other people on the road. I see people valuing life at work. At the hospital I see patients who are fighting for their lives and doctors, nurses, and other health-care professionals who have dedicated themselves to saving lives. People often commiserate about the news they watch on the TV or read in the newspaper. They talk about how terrible it is that a murder happened so close to home or that a shooter came in and randomly shot children. The news of death leaves us with heavy hearts, and the devastation shows on our faces.

But when does life begin? Is it conception? Is it a heartbeat? Is it brain function? Is it being viable outside the womb? Is it birth? Ever since the ruling of *Roe v. Wade* in 1973, this has been a heated and emotional debate with the focal point being the moment at which life begins. Medical capability has advanced, politics have changed, presidents have come and gone, but the debate over when life begins continues. Now that

Roe v. Wade has been overturned and laws about abortion are in the hands of individual states, there are many new arguments about whether life in the womb should be protected by law and when that protection should be required. The debate is as heated as ever.

Let's take a moment and look at this from a medical and logical standpoint. With the current technology, a heartbeat can be detected via vaginal ultrasound as early as six weeks after conception. At work, I deliver lifesaving CPR if a patient's heart stops beating. During a code (when a patient in unresponsive and CPR is required), the shortest amount of time I have seen a medical team working on a patient is 20 minutes. That's 20 minutes of a patient without a heartbeat and trained professionals delivering compressions, artificial breaths, high-energy shocks, and lifesaving medication, all with the intention of saving a life. This can last closer to an hour, and it's exhausting in every sense of the word. If a patient chooses not to receive CPR and the heart stops beating, a doctor listens for a heartbeat for a minute and pronounces a patient dead if no heartbeat is found. Medically, the presence or absence of a heartbeat defines life. Logically, shouldn't that be the same for a baby in the womb? If a heartbeat can be detected at six weeks in the womb, by medical definition wouldn't that child be alive?

But so many people don't see what I see. If we as a society still can't agree when life begins, we clearly can't rely on the opinions of sinful people. So what does God, the Creator of life, say? He tells us that from the moment of conception, he knew us, he loved us, and he had a plan to save us. That sounds like life to me.

What does God say about life? He says I was knit in my mother's womb:

> You created my inmost being; you knit me together in my mother's womb. I praise you because I am fearfully and wonderfully made; your works are wonderful, I know that full well. My frame was not hidden from you when I was made in the secret place, when I was woven together in the depths of the earth. Your eyes saw my unformed body; all the days ordained for me were written in your book before one of them came to be. (Psalm 139:13-16)

God tells us that he made us and we belong to him. "Know that the LORD is God. It is he who made us, and we are his; we are his people, the sheep of his pasture" (Psalm 100:3).

It is so comforting to know that God thought of me individually while forming me in my mother's womb. That with the proof of a beating heart so early on leads me to believe that babies inside the womb are lives to be loved and cherished. That would make abortion wrong.

What if you have had an abortion or have encouraged someone to have an abortion? The awesome thing about Jesus is that he still loves you and forgives you. He died once and for all on the cross for the sins of all people, no matter how bad or ugly they seem.

> There is now no condemnation for those who are in Christ Jesus, because through Christ Jesus the law of the Spirit who gives life has set you free from the law of sin and death. For what the law was powerless to do because it was weakened by the flesh, God did by sending his own Son in the likeness of sinful flesh to be a sin offering. (Romans 8:1-3)

> In him we have redemption through his blood, the forgiveness of sins, in accordance with the riches of God's grace. (Ephesians 1:7)

No sin is too great for God to forgive. As God's children, nothing can separate us from his love and compassion.

> As high as the heavens are above the earth, so great is his love for those who fear him; as far as the east is from the west, so far has he removed our transgressions from us. As a father has compassion on his children, so the LORD has compassion on those who fear him. (Psalm 103:11-13)

I am sure you have known someone in your life who claimed to be a Christian but did not act in a very Christianlike way. There may be a person you know who preaches pro-life in a demeaning and hurtful manner, putting people down and shaming them. I would be turned off to the message from that person who did not treat me with dignity or respect or approach the topic with gentleness, like Jesus says to do. The pro-life message can be pushed aside because of the way in which it is conveyed.

I just want to remind you that we are all sinful. We are imperfect people trying to convey a message, but we often fall short of the correct motivation and delivery. I have been pro-life my whole life because of what the Bible says, but I can understand how someone would be turned off to the message because of the manner in which it is preached.

Perhaps people appear to be unsympathetic to the rape victim and indifferent to helping mothers who have had an abortion or offering help to mothers who have chosen life. Instead of showing criticism, judgment, and cruelty, let us show respect, love, and forgiveness. Pray for mothers and their partners who are deciding if they should choose life. Pray for those who have chosen an abortion that they would seek forgiveness and that the Lord would comfort them. Pray for those who have chosen life and are now struggling to make ends meet. Reach out to help them if you can. Pray for those who are witnessing but are not doing it gracefully. Finally, pray that your eyes will be opened to the truth in God's Word, because in there you will find saving truth.

How wonderful it is that God protected Rachel and Amy and put them in their particular families. Thank God that their parents chose life. We as Christians need to let struggling mothers know that God will help and guide them no matter what challenges come their way.

Unanswered Whys

Visited my Grandma today—my only grandparent left on both my side and Ben's side. She's 91 years old, going on 92 in a couple of months. [Day 3 of 180]

Through journaling, I discovered I've already been waiting on God and in some instances for a long time. Two similar circumstances made me wonder again why things happen as they do, and both made me see that only God knows the answer.

The more my grandmother ages here on this earth (she was 91 years old when I was writing this), the more forgetful she becomes. But one thing she always remembers to bring up—between the repeated conversations on how delicious the broccoli soup is and how hot it is outside—is her youngest son. She talks about how it's not fair that he went to heaven before she did.

Now that I have a son of my own, I can relate even more to Grandma's situation. I have to admit that my uncle dying before Grandma almost seems wrong or backward to me too. Why should the young be cut short while the old linger on? It's hard for our puny little brains to wrap our heads around God's timing. It just doesn't add up with human logic.

But I must remember that my thoughts are not God's thoughts and his ways are not my ways (Isaiah 55:8,9). That is kind of comforting. I don't always have it figured out, but God does. So while I wait on God to show me his timing, I've had to work on learning that his timing may always be a mystery on this earth. I guess it has to be that way because his ways are beyond what I know or think is right. For some answers, God will keep me waiting until I'm in heaven.

Another very trying moment was when a friend received a phone call in my presence telling her that her teenage son had taken his own life. Two things happened among those who were there. We all wanted right away to tell our families that we loved them, and, more importantly, we all wanted to pray. In the moment, I was overcome with the feeling that what we needed most was God. I asked everyone there if it was okay with them if I said a quick prayer, to which they all nodded in agreement.

I can't remember exactly what I said. All I know is I prayed that God would give my friend and her family comfort and peace.

Timing. It just does not make any sense at all that a son would leave this earth before his mother. It doesn't make sense that a beloved son would take his own life. We don't know the reasons for it. We all know it is inevitable that everyone on this earth is going to die, but we can't understand why it happens like this.

I know the devil works overtime in situations like these. He crawls into the corners of our brains to create doubt in God and cause us to think thoughts like "How could this happen if there's a loving God?" I don't know what thoughts my grandma and my friend were thinking, but putting myself in their shoes, I'd probably be thinking something along the lines of "This isn't fair. God should have taken me first." The devil is smart and capitalizes on the sinfulness of this world to create more doubt and sin. God does not want us to use our own experience or logic to rationalize what happens but, rather, to lean completely on him and to trust in his plan. "Trust in the LORD with all your heart and lean not on your own understanding; in all your ways submit to him, and he will make your paths straight" (Proverbs 3:5,6). Can God really make a straight path through such bitter grief and shock? Yes, he can!

Two Bible passages come to mind in regard to strength and peace during unthinkable times:

> So do not fear, for I am with you; do not be dismayed, for I am your God. I will strengthen you and help you; I will uphold you with my righteous right hand. (Isaiah 41:10)

> I am convinced that neither death nor life, neither angels nor demons, neither the present nor the future, nor any powers, neither height nor depth, nor anything else in all creation, will be able to separate us from the love of God that is in Christ Jesus our Lord. (Romans 8:38,39)

I am unsure of my friend's faith or of her son's, but I take hope in the biblical account of the thief who was crucified next to Jesus. During some of his last moments on earth, before he died on the cross next to Jesus, he recognized his sinfulness. He recognized his own brokenness and guilt before God. He believed that the man hanging on the cross next to him was his Savior and the King of heaven. In the world's eyes, the thief died damned and worthless, but the thief died in great peace. He knew he was going to enter heaven because Jesus' words filled him with hope: "Today you will be with me in paradise."

Below is the full and powerful account of the thief's change of heart:

> One of the criminals who hung there hurled insults at him: "Aren't you the Messiah? Save yourself and us!"
>
> But the other criminal rebuked him. "Don't you fear God," he said, "since you are under the same sentence? We are punished justly, for we are getting what our deeds deserve. But this man has done nothing wrong."
>
> Then he said, "Jesus, remember me when you come into your kingdom."
>
> Jesus answered him, "Truly I tell you, today you will be with me in paradise." (Luke 23:39-43)

I pray that mothers who lose their children will not have long to wait before their hearts are filled with peace.

TRAVEL TIPS: Roadblocks

The devil is smart, active, and present in our daily lives more than we'd like to think. He's working hard to come up with excuses on why you should not begin your own 180 journey. A decline in health, a family drama, and a change in jobs are challenges the devil capitalizes on and uses to create doubt that you are able to fit time for God into your schedule. From our point of view, there is no perfect time to begin a 180 journey, but God's timing for our lives is always perfect. Life is never going to be perfect, so why not commit now to your 180? Perhaps by beginning a 180 journey you will be able to see God more in whatever waiting you may have in your life in the next six months.

Frozen

Have you ever had one of those questions that sort of just freezes you where you are?

I had a patient with an extremely large open wound to his neck area caused by his head and neck cancer. It was infected and had a strong malodorous smell. He was admitted to the hospital for wound care and pain management.

It was determined through many discussions that no further treatment options were available for the patient, meaning no more chemotherapy or radiation. This meant that the best option for him was to go to a care center that could take care of his pain and wound care needs. He was not safe to go home because he was not independent enough. He couldn't manage the activities of daily living, not to mention his wound care that needed to be done twice per day.

Sometimes the patient became confused or forgetful. He communicated via writing on a sheet of paper, since his tracheostomy—another result of his advanced cancer—made him unable to talk. One day he wrote on the sheet of paper asking when he was going home. That question took me by surprise because the medical team had been updating him with their plan. Despite those many conversations, he believed it would just be a matter of time before he was able to return home. His question froze me. I had to pause and think how to best answer his question. Was there some way to do it gently? I explained to him once again where he was going and why he was going there, just like the doctors had done. He seemed saddened by my answer. It looked like I had shattered his dreams.

Sometimes the powerlessness I see in my patients' faces reminds me of my own powerlessness, which helps me realize even more how powerful God really is. Through my 180 journey, I've learned more than ever that I cannot do anything apart from God and I need to wait on God more to show me his power and grace. He may show that power by some dramatic act of restoration or help, or he may show it by giving me peace, peace that can guard my heart even when my situation looks hopeless. He says, "Do not be anxious about anything, but in every situation, by prayer and petition, with thanksgiving, present your requests to God. And the peace of God, which transcends all understanding, will guard your hearts and your minds in Christ Jesus" (Philippians 4:6,7).

And what about all the waiting the patient has to go through? He has to wait in the hospital for who knows how long until the social worker and his family figure out a place for him to live. He has to wait to meet his new caregivers at the facility and learn how to adjust to the rhythm of his new home. He has to wait for his pain meds and daily dressing changes. He has to wait for the nurses for assistance. I'm not sure if my patient believes in God, but I hope and pray that this patient has found peace, the true peace only God can offer, in his day-to-day waiting.

YOUR TURN

- Have you ever had to face disease or sickness in a close family member or friend? How did you cope?

- How did you or your loved one get to show faith to those surrounding him or her?

- How do you comfort those who are sick? Do you bring Jesus into the conversation?

- Do you find yourself waiting on God more when there is a crisis in your life, such as worrying over a sick loved one?

TRAVEL TIPS: Reflection

It is enough work just to keep journaling every day, but to really get the most out of your journaling, it is good to make time to reread what you have written. Taking time to reflect on your journaling/praying/Bible studies helps you refocus on your journey. How often should you reread? It might be worthwhile at the end of each week to skim over that week's entries. At least take time to pause at day 60, 120, and 180, I would say. Here are some questions you might keep in mind as you revisit where you've been on your journey:

○ What have you learned during each time frame?

○ How have your thoughts on the topic evolved?

○ Has the journey become easier or more difficult?

○ Have you been noticing others around you living out (or maybe not living out) your topic?

Waiting on God Means Doing Right Even When It Feels All Wrong

Hurry up and Wait

My patient has waited days to get his gastric-tube placed. [Day 4 of 180]

I've had to realize how much waiting we do in everyday life.

Working in a hospital setting almost exclusively with veterans, the phrase "Hurry up and wait" is one that is said almost as much as "How are you doing today?" I receive a phone call that the surgical team is ready for my patient's surgery and wants me to get him to the OR stat. I rush around and assist him into a gown and help him onto a gurney made up with fresh linens. Right when the escort arrives to transport my patient to his procedure, my phone rings again. It's the OR explaining that there has been another emergency and my patient's procedure has been bumped to a later time. Hurry up and wait.

I arrive at the airport two hours prior to the departure time like I'm supposed to. I get through security in 11 minutes and now must sit and wait for takeoff. On top of that, my flight is delayed 20 minutes. Hurry up and wait.

I leave work later than expected. Now I feel like I have to speed most of the way to my doctor's appointment so I'm not late. When I arrive, I am pleased to find out I am only two minutes late. The receptionist politely tells me that my doctor is running behind about 20 minutes. Once again, hurry up and wait.

Appointments, daily tasks, and events in life often force us into this hurry-up-and-wait mentality, and it seems from my patients that this is especially true in the military. The truth is that too often when it comes to my spiritual life, I resent that God makes me hurry up and wait. I fall into this mentality that I am rushing through life trying to do *my* part, only to find out that God's answer is wait. Then I get disheartened.

This disappointment could be curbed if all along I would put my faith and trust in God, that he knows what is best and understands my life better than I do. When the waiting comes from God's hand, hurry up and wait isn't a bad thing. The real question is, am I waiting to get *my* way, believing it must be best, or waiting for God to get *his* way, believing it must be best?

> I wait for the Lord, my whole being waits,
> and in his word I put my hope.
> I wait for the Lord
> more than watchmen wait for the morning.
> (Psalm 130:5,6)

I've always enjoyed reading the book of Psalms. If there were nights during my 180 when I wanted to read, but I was too tired to concentrate on a heavier book (like maybe from the Old Testament), I would read a psalm instead. Here is another section from Scripture—again from Psalms—that gave me confidence when the days seemed long or it felt like God wasn't answering my requests on my timeline.

> I remain confident of this:
> I will see the goodness of the Lord
> in the land of the living.
> Wait for the Lord;
> be strong and take heart
> and wait for the Lord. (Psalm 27:13,14)

Waiting can wear us down, but what really wears us thin is waiting on our own accord without God. Without God, we struggle to stay strong. Without God, we become bogged down with everyday mistakes, regrets, and what-ifs. But God wants us to come to him, to hope in him, and he promises that he will give us strength.

> He gives strength to the weary
> and increases the power of the weak.
> Even youths grow tired and weary,
> and young men stumble and fall;
> but those who hope in the LORD
> will renew their strength.
> They will soar on wings like eagles;
> they will run and not grow weary,
> they will walk and not be faint. (Isaiah 40:29-31)

Through my daily personal Bible study, I was often overtaken with thoughts of gratitude. God really used my time in the Bible to strengthen me to wait for him. He reassured me that he will be good to me even when the waiting doesn't feel good. He quieted my impatience. He helped me believe his promises like this one:

> The LORD is good to those whose hope is in him,
> to the one who seeks him;
> it is good to wait quietly
> for the salvation of the LORD. (Lamentations 3:25,26)

Then there is the biggest hurry up and wait: waiting for heaven. Waiting for Jesus to come back and fix everything, to come back and take us home. As Christians, we should always be waiting for the Lord's return. Jesus urges us to keep ourselves ready for him:

> Be dressed ready for service and keep your lamps burn-
> ing, like servants waiting for their master to return from
> a wedding banquet, so that when he comes and knocks
> they can immediately open the door for him. It will be
> good for those servants whose master finds them watch-
> ing when he comes. Truly I tell you, he will dress him-
> self to serve, will have them recline at the table and will
> come and wait on them. (Luke 12:35-37)

This concept took a while for me during my 180 journey to really start to understand. At first I thought that waiting on God was mostly just learning to be more patient, learning to give control over to him. But so many of the passages in the New Testament (the part of the Bible written after Jesus came) that use the word *wait* are about waiting for Jesus to come back. In Luke's gospel, Jesus was urging his disciples to watch for his return, to be ready for him at any moment, "Be dressed ready for service and keep your lamps burning." I'm still working on this being a focus in my everyday life. Focusing on heaven as my ultimate goal and telling others of his grace—I know that this should be on the forefront of my heart and mind. This mindset would have me thinking about what really matters in life: my salvation and the salvation of others. It's as simple as that.

Waiting for Jesus does not mean just sitting on my front porch, twiddling my thumbs, and staring at the sky. Yes, waiting for Jesus means keeping ready for his return by keeping my heart full of the news that he is my Savior. It also means I don't just sit on this good news, but I hurry up and *spread* that story of Jesus' love. There is a passage in the Bible, written by Jesus' friend Peter, that I have on my heart sometimes but not often enough: "In your hearts revere Christ as Lord. Always be prepared to give an answer to everyone who asks you to give the reason for the hope that you have. But do this with gentleness and respect" (1 Peter 3:15).

Revere: a deep respect or admiration for something. This word couldn't ring truer in my relationship with Christ. I revere him, and that makes me want to learn everything I can about him in the Bible. And God doesn't want me to talk just to people who are easy or I know will be receptive to the gospel, but he wants me to witness to *everyone*. And it's not just under certain fair-weather conditions but *always*. It doesn't always feel like the right time to talk about Jesus. It often feels like that kind of conversation could wait until later. But then I'm acting like Jesus isn't coming soon, like I think he will be "a long time in coming" (Luke 12:45). I want to be found sharing Jesus' love with others whenever he returns. When I look up online the phrase "the time is short," one of the first search results is a sermon from some time ago by the preacher Billy Graham. In it he says these challenging words:

> We could use millions of people marching for Christ
> all over the world right now, taking love instead of hate

to the world, telling the people how to be saved, telling them how they can find forgiveness and newness of life. ("The Time Is Short: A Classic Message from Billy Graham," Billy Graham Evangelistic Association of Canada, billygraham.ca/stories/the-time-is-short-a-classic-message-from-billy-graham)

Jesus said, "I have brought you glory on earth by finishing the work you gave me to do" (John 17:4). God has given you something to do too. Are you working on it? Have you finished it? You don't have much time. You never know how long you have to live. That's the reason the Bible says, "Prepare to meet your God" (Amos 4:12). Be ready at all times. "Be ready, because the Son of Man will come at an hour when you do not expect him" (Matthew 24:44). The time is urgent. Don't waste it.

Waiting on Jesus' return means not waiting to spread his love but hurrying to do so. Hurrying with all "gentleness and respect" for the people we talk with, as Peter says, but still hurrying. I guess this is the biggest hurry up and wait.

Boldly Witness

Instead of focusing on how hard they've been practicing or how nervous they were, they turned it back to Christ. [Day 44 of 180]

As I have mentioned before, the Olympics are well loved in our home. One night in August, Ben and I were enjoying the 2016 Rio Olympics and watching the synchronized diving event. During the interviews following an outstanding silver medal performance, David Boudia and Steele Johnson, two US Olympic divers, gave God one hundred percent of the glory. Ben and I loved it. Instead of focusing on how hard they had been practicing or how nervous they were, they turned it back to Christ. When David Boudia commented on the enormous pressure of the Olympics, he stated,

> I just think the past week, there's just been an enormous amount of pressure, and I've felt it. You know, it's just an identity crisis. When my mind is on this, thinking I'm defined by this, then my mind goes crazy, but we both know our identity is in Christ.

Steele Johnson chimed in,

> The fact that I was going into this event knowing that my identity is rooted in Christ—and not what the result of this competition is—just gave me peace. It gave me ease, and it let me enjoy the contest. If something went great, I was happy. If something didn't go great, I could still find joy because I'm at the Olympics.

Here were two US Olympic divers proclaiming Jesus' name to people watching the Olympics all over the world. What an amazing way to use the talents God has given them as a platform to be witnesses of Christ to the millions of viewers watching the live interview. What an inspiration. You can still watch their post-performance interview online.

In 2021, Steele Johnson withdrew from the Olympic trials because of an ongoing foot injury. Despite his sadness over not being able to compete, he maintained his faith that God was in control and his certainty of his identity in Christ. He professed his faith in his victory as well as in his defeat. It's a lesson we all can learn. (You can read his statement on his Instagram profile.)

Sometimes it sounds best to wait on God to present an opportunity for witnessing. It's not wrong to wait on God for the golden opportunity, but God also wants us to seek out those opportunities of witnessing and not idly wait. Maybe we are waiting for the perfect person on a perfectly sunny day who we know will respond in a courteous manner. No, God calls us to be ready "in season and out of season" (2 Timothy 4:2), to be in the trenches, and to step out in faith. David Boudia and Steele Johnson stepped out in faith in front of millions of viewers, and in a very natural way they shared the comfort and peace they had in Jesus.

The divers' witnessing came *from* their waiting on Jesus. It wasn't like they decided after the dive to talk about Jesus. They had been filling their minds with their identity in Christ all along. "The mouth speaks what the heart is full of" (Luke 6:45). They had filled their hearts with Christ, waiting on him more than waiting for a medal. Christ naturally then came out of their mouths.

Paul encourages us believers in his letter to Timothy, "The Spirit God gave us does not make us timid, but gives us power, love and self-discipline" (2 Timothy 1:7).

Notice the word *timid*. The Spirit of God does not make us timid. That's because when the Spirit is working within us, it's not our power or strength but the Holy Spirit's. God is the one who is propelling "power, love and self-discipline," not us.

In Paul's second letter to Timothy, he tells him, "So do not be ashamed of the testimony about our Lord or of me his prisoner. Rather, join with me in suffering for the gospel, by the power of God" (2 Timothy 1:8).

I know I struggle with confidently sharing the good news with others. It's a scary thing because I don't know how people are going to respond or treat me afterward. But God promises he will get me through with his power when sharing my faith does not go so well.

He has saved us and called us to a holy life—not because of anything we have done but because of his own purpose and grace. This grace was given us in Christ Jesus before the beginning of time, but it has now been revealed through the appearing of our Savior, Christ Jesus, who has destroyed death and has brought life and immortality to light through the gospel. (2 Timothy 1:9,10)

How powerful is this saving truth! How freeing to hear about "Christ Jesus, who has destroyed death and has brought *life* and *immortality* to *light* through the gospel." Jesus brought life and light to the world, a place where there is nothing truly good apart from Christ. "That is why I am suffering as I am. Yet this is no cause for shame, because I know whom I have believed, and am convinced that he is able to guard what I have entrusted to him until that day" (2 Timothy 1:12).

What a reminder: Spreading the gospel is such a priceless labor that we can rejoice no matter how we must suffer for it. Paul entrusted his safety, privacy, and personal comfort to Jesus, and he was *waiting* for Jesus' return knowing it was all worth it.

Unfortunately, many Christians across the globe face violence and persecution for their faith. This is something uncomfortable to think about and something I like to block out of my mind and try not to think about. But every so often it puts me on my hands and knees at night, thankful that as a Christian in the US I can proclaim my beliefs, and I also pray for those who live in fear of violent persecution on a regular basis.

Citizens of the US are blessed. Freedom of speech. Freedom of religion. Why wouldn't we share the gospel? Are we afraid of what others might think of us? Are we afraid that we may come off as if we think we're better than others or a goody-two-shoes? Are we afraid our friends will think we're weird and won't want to hang with us anymore? Martin Luther expressed something similar, writing about John 17:15.

There is so much great, shameful ingratitude and contempt in the world, and such terrible blasphemy and persecution of God's Word besides, that a pious preacher is finally loathe to preach another word. God could do nothing to please us better than to take us away soon, so that we neither see nor hear this calamity. But what shall we do? . . . Though we join all heads and hands, it will require effort and labor to preserve the Word among even a few, to keep the Word that it might not utterly perish and all people go to the devil. (Martin Luther, *What Luther Says: An Anthology,* compiled by Ewald M. Plass, St. Louis: Concordia Publishing House, 1959, p. 1121)

We have these same fears. But God calls us to "not be ashamed of the testimony" and "join with [Paul and other Christian martyrs] in suffering for the gospel" (2 Timothy 1:8). No matter what happens, we have our inheritance in heaven that can't be taken away from us. That is what we should be waiting for more than the approval of others. Waiting for Jesus to bring us "life and immortality" is the Spirit's cure for timidity (2 Timothy 1:10).

I pray that I wait on God more this way, waiting for him to show me frequent opportunities to use my God-given talents in everyday life to witness about Christ. May God give each of us the boldness and hopefulness we need—like David Boudia and Steele Johnson—to reach those people in our lives who need Christ.

YOUR TURN

- Have you boldly witnessed Christ to others recently?
- What roadblocks are in the way of boldly witnessing?
- What are you waiting for God to present to you in order to perfectly witness?

Witnessing

What does it mean to be a witness? It means sharing what you have seen, observed, or heard. What does it mean to be a witness in the Christian sense? It means sharing what you read in the Bible (God-inspired content) and what you know and believe is true.

Not only are Christians called to witness, but they also are called to "be prepared to give an answer to everyone who asks [them] to give the reason for the hope that [they] have" (1 Peter 3:15). Sharing God's Word could lead to further questions. God wants us to be prepared, and what better way to be prepared than to be immersed in his Word frequently. God even tells us the demeanor in which we should witness: "with gentleness and respect" (1 Peter 3:15).

Christians witnessing for Christ can become caught up in acting like a jury or a judge, but we are simply called by God to be witnesses, not judges. We cannot judge a person's heart; only the almighty God can. We are called to share God's love and leave the work of faith to the Holy Spirit.

I am a Christian and know I am saved; do I really have to witness to others? The answer is yes. God commands it: "Go into all the world and preach the gospel to all creation" (Mark 16:15). I'm sure I have come up with every excuse in the book as to why it's too hard to witness: I'm too young. It's not the right opportunity. I won't have the right words to say or the correct tone. God equipped Jeremiah to witness: "You must go to everyone I send you to and say whatever I command you. Do not be afraid of them, for I am with you and will rescue you" (Jeremiah 1:7,8). In the same way, God also equips all believers. How comforting to know that God will rescue me. This reminder takes the pressure off me to say everything perfectly. It brings the conversation back to Jesus and what he says to be true, knowing my strength does not come from my own merit but, rather, from God. And what or whom should I fear? "I am not ashamed of the gospel, because it is the power of God that brings salvation to everyone who believes: first to the Jew, then to the Gentile" (Romans 1:16).

Not only does God command me to witness, but I should be so excited about the good news of Christ that I am anxious to witness to others. In the Bible, God often talks about Christians as the light of the earth. It's a very clear image to me that Christians naturally should want to share the awesome news that all are saved because of Jesus' death on the cross. God talks about this analogy in Matthew 5:14b-16:

> A town built on a hill cannot be hidden. Neither do people light a lamp and put it under a bowl. Instead

they put it on its stand, and it gives light to everyone in the house. In the same way, let your light shine before others, that they may see your good deeds and glorify your Father in heaven.

The apostle Paul, the former persecutor of Christians turned on-fire preacher of Christ crucified, sums up the above thoughts of witnessing perfectly:

> Devote yourselves to prayer, being watchful and thankful. And pray for us, too, that God may open a door for our message, so that we may proclaim the mystery of Christ, for which I am in chains. Pray that I may proclaim it clearly, as I should. Be wise in the way you act toward outsiders; make the most of every opportunity. Let your conversation be always full of grace, seasoned with salt, so that you may know how to answer everyone. (Colossians 4:2-6)

Whenever I read this section, I often linger on the words "let your conversation be always full of grace." This does not always happen for me, so what a great reminder it is to have. I think people new to God's grace might listen to me more intently if they see me *living* a life full of God's grace.

In the World, Not *of* the World

> If the world hates you, keep in mind that it hated me
> first. If you belonged to the world, it would love you as
> its own. As it is, you do not belong to the world, but I
> have chosen you out of the world. That is why the world
> hates you. Remember what I told you: "A servant is not
> greater than his master." If they persecuted me, they will
> persecute you also. If they obeyed my teaching, they will
> obey yours also. They will treat you this way because of
> my name, for they do not know the one who sent me.
> (John 15:18-21)

I know this truth so well: the command to be in the world and not of the
world. It's one thing to know it and another thing to act on it. At work,
parties, or gatherings, there are conversations I am not comfortable with
because I know God is not comfortable with them. But at times I don't
do anything. I don't pretend it's all good and jump in on the conversation,
but I also don't change the subject or try to steer the conversation in a
better direction. I am a wallflower in the room, just letting these disgrace-
ful conversations happen. I know I need to speak up, but I also know I
don't want to be the weird one at the gathering, not "fun enough" or
"cut loose" enough.

Be in the world, not of the world. Jesus says that others may hate me
for following him, but he reminds me that others hated him first. What
is truly the worst that can happen? They would likely not harm me or
throw me in prison. They might reject my friendship, they might harm
my good name, or they might convince other friends not to talk to me.
This would be hard, no doubt, but not the worst thing. It is comforting to know that I have a large group of Christian family members and
friends to back me up. Even if I didn't have such a large support system,
I have Christ, and that is enough.

> Then Jesus said to his disciples, "Whoever wants to be
> my disciple must deny themselves and take up their cross
> and follow me. For whoever wants to save their life will
> lose it, but whoever loses their life for me will find it.

What good will it be for someone to gain the whole world, yet forfeit their soul? Or what can anyone give in exchange for their soul? For the Son of Man is going to come in his Father's glory with his angels, and then he will reward each person according to what they have done." (Matthew 16:24-27)

Jesus commands his people to lose their lives for him. I'm not talking about seeking out martyrdom. I'm talking about letting go of my desires that feed what I want. Letting go of what the world wants me to be and letting God take over every aspect of my life, even the areas of my life that are hard to let go. He wants me to take on my new identity in Christ. He even goes as far as to say that if we gain the whole world but have to give up our souls or our salvation, it's not worth it.

I remember my fourth summer at Camp Phillip serving as junior staff director. At times I felt guilty that I was working there for yet another summer. My parents love me a ton and want the best for me, and that summer they wanted me to work at a hospital as a nursing assistant or intern so that I could prepare myself for my career postgraduation. I understood where they were coming from, but I just felt convinced that I should return to camp, that my time and my calling there were not supposed to end quite yet. Still, I ended up feeling badly that I wasn't doing what my nursing friends were doing or what my parents thought was best for me. It was really tough at the time, and I felt torn. Was I making a stupid or selfish decision by not interning in a hospital? Would I ever find a job postgraduation?

I remember early that summer talking to my boss, telling him about these guilty and conflicted feelings. He recommended writing a letter to my parents explaining what made me so sure I was meant to serve at Camp Phillip that summer. This led me to realize that I had never really explained to my parents my passion for camp and my desire to serve there. After some thought, I wrote to them. I remember quoting the verse above from Matthew, reminding them (and, more importantly, myself) why this was the right decision. I knew I wasn't doing the right worldly thing, the right move for my future career, but I was losing myself to God. I was able to pour my heart into my camp work more than I could have as a nursing intern. It was my second year directing the junior staff with Ben, and God blessed us. We worked out so many of the kinks from how we had done things the previous year. We knew each other's strengths so much better that we could capitalize on them. We made it one truly unforgettable summer serving side by side.

I learned a lesson that summer about stepping back from the pressures of this world and doing what's most important to further God's kingdom.

Then despite having zero hospital work experience, God still blessed me to find my career. Before I had even graduated from nursing school, I landed a job at the VA Hospital—one of six new graduates selected for a one-year prestigious and competitive nurse residency program. Landing a career, especially a very covetous position, is nothing short of a blessing straight from God. I never expected to find a job so quickly with my lack of experience. Don't get me wrong; I was still worried during the job hunt, and feelings of doubt crept in. But God carried me through. After the residency, I was hired full-time on the unit that was my first choice, the inpatient medicine/oncology unit, and I've been there ever since. I feel so blessed by the journey that has led me this far and using my nursing degree to serve veterans, who deserve the best care.

My 180 had me reflecting on these things, reflecting on how I got to where I am today. It wasn't about luck or "I deserved it because I worked so hard." Rather, I can see God clearly through it all, directing me always. Along the way as I made school choices and career plans, sometimes I was waiting on God and other times I was taking things into my own hands. In his love, God was there through it all. I can look back and see that I grew more and had more peace when I was waiting on God and depending on him.

YOUR TURN

- When have you trusted God in his timing and clung to his promises instead of conforming to the world's standards and expectations?

Not of the World, but *Into* the World

I went into my job as a nurse thinking, "This is just going to be a job. I don't have to become friends with my coworkers. I plan to just put in my time and come home." This may sound cold or cynical, but allow me to explain.

As I have mentioned in other chapters, before I graduated and started my job as a full-time registered nurse (RN), I had worked the four previous summers at a Christian summer camp in Wisconsin. Those four summers were the best. The first two summers I was a camp counselor, spending days in the sun teaching little kids about Jesus, leading games, singing camp songs, and cooling off in the crystal clear lake. The last two summers I had the privilege of serving alongside my boyfriend (now my husband) as directors of the junior staff, the high school volunteers. Camp is where I learned a lot about myself and grew most as a person. I learned how to be a leader. I learned that I'm capable of a lot more than I thought I was. I learned that serving God is real and tangible and living for him isn't something I should be afraid to do. I had the best boss who truly cared for me and every person on his staff. Every summer he sat down with me and helped me make both personal growth and job-related goals to challenge me. The other bonuses of my work included meeting my husband at camp, gaining the best friends a girl could ask for, and making memories to last a lifetime.

When I started my hospital job, I knew going into it that I wasn't going to have a boss like the one at camp, the boss who spent hours setting goals and evaluating with me. I also assumed that my boss wasn't looking to be my friend. I knew that I wasn't going to get a tan or breathe fresh air all day (rather, recycled hospital air). I knew we would not start staff meetings with prayer and I wouldn't receive letters of encouragement from my coworkers. I understood this new, real-life job was going to be different, but the new job wasn't really the problem. It was my attitude. Day after day I was comparing the jobs, getting down on how the nursing job didn't even come close to how great my camp job was. I still realized the gravity of my new job. I had a sense of how special my experiences as a nurse could be, but I just wasn't looking at them with the right frame of mind. I seriously lacked appreciation and contentment.

It took me at least a year of working as a nurse to see the new blessings right in front of me. I realized I had been blind to many of the new opportunities at my RN job. Yes, they are very different opportunities from what I had at camp, but in a good way. God was patiently showing me how to love my job and to love how he wants me to serve him right now. God has put me here to hold the hands of dying veterans for him. God has put me here to listen to heartbroken people who just can't kick their drinking habit because it's their only "escape" from their horrific memories of war. God has put me here to make new friends with a diverse group of coworkers who aren't necessarily Christians but who need the Christian love and hope that I can share. None of these are opportunities I would have had if I had stayed in my safe camp bubble. Jesus doesn't just call us to be not *of* the world. He also sends us *into* the world. Talking to his Father about his followers, Jesus said, "My prayer is not that you take them out of the world but that you protect them. . . . They are not of the world, even as I am not of it. As you sent me into the world, I have sent them into the world" (John 17:15,16,18).

This quote from a blog post I came across, talking about these same words of Jesus, really hits home for me:

> Notice that for Jesus being "not of the world" isn't the destination in these verses but the starting place. . . . He is not of the world, and he begins by saying that his followers are not of the world. But it's going somewhere. Jesus is not huddling up the team for another round of *Kumbaya*, but so that we can run the next play and advance the ball down the field.
>
> The accent falls on being sent, with a mission, to the world—not being mainly on a mission to disassociate from this world . . . we are sent into the world on [a] mission for gospel advance through disciple making.
>
> Jesus's true followers have not only been crucified to the world, but also raised to new life and sent back in to

free others. We've been rescued from the darkness and given the Light not merely to flee the darkness, but to guide our steps as we go back in to rescue others. (David Mathis, "Let's Revise the Popular Phrase: 'In But Not Of,' " desiringgod.org)

I had a talk with my friend Rachel (the one who was adopted from Colombia) about the relationships I've built with my great coworkers and how my conversations with them have at times crossed over to God. Whether it's talking about where I go to church, sharing what God has been doing for the people in my life, or showing his sympathy as I lend a listening ear to a coworker in need, it has been a blessing to see the walls crumble down and to learn not to be ashamed.

Rachel said it best, "Isn't it crazy how God uses imperfect people like us to witness to his perfection?" Yes, it sure is.

When I was first asked to be a part of this series, I thought, "Why me?" The more I prayed and pondered this request, the more I came to realize it isn't ME that people need to read about, but it's about Jesus. My 180 journey is about me pointing to Jesus, not just in this book but in everything I do and everywhere I am. It's about waiting on Jesus to show me opportunities to introduce people to him even when I'm not at camp. And finally, it's about waiting for him to come back and catch me talking to others about him.

Epilogue

Is your cup of coffee cold? Are you still sitting in your favorite spot?

My prayer is that the stories I've shared with you have been worthwhile, that you get a glimpse into my life and clearly see the ways in which I have been learning to wait on God more, and that perhaps you have taken notice of the ways you have or have not been waiting on God. You may not have any experiences like mine, but I hope my stories made you think. I hope they made you reflect on your own experiences that may teach you to wait on God more. No matter what experiences we have, let us work toward leaning on God, waiting for him to hold us up, because without him as our rock we will not stand. Let's not be ashamed of talking about the Savior, whose glorious return we are waiting for. We can start by talking about this book, what we have learned about waiting on God more, and why he is totally worth waiting for.

My challenge to you is to embark on your own 180 journey focusing on waiting on God more. Set a goal for yourself and stick to it. Find an accountability partner who will check in on you—and even better, complete the challenge with you. Will it take time, focus, and dedication? Absolutely. But I know that God will answer your prayers and meet you in his Word—you and your partner! Make sure to share the experience with someone who not only helps you stay on task but also helps you process all your experiences, put them into words, and profit from them in your spiritual life.

If this book inspires at least one person, I would be grateful, but even if no one picks it up or turns a single page, I still consider it a personal success. I've learned and grown so much through the process that it almost seems like someone reading my book is a secondary goal. My faith has been greatly strengthened. I have learned how to be patient in the waiting and have peace in the outcome. I've learned more easily to notice God's presence in the waiting with my eyes and ears. I've learned to remember that everything in life has a purpose, even if I don't know what that purpose is yet.

The truth of the matter is that I would love to say I've completed my 180, that I've turned 180 degrees in the other direction from impatience and self-reliance and no longer have any problems waiting on God. That is not the case. I'm still a work in progress, struggling with God's timing. I still fail to notice his grace around me and the blessings he has placed in my life. I'm still waiting on God to show me contentment in motherhood. I'm still waiting on God to give relief and comfort to struggling loved ones. I'm still waiting on God to answer the whys about certain people in my life who have serious illnesses and problems. Waiting, waiting, and more waiting.

When Ben and I first got married, I earned the nickname Maverick from him. I would make a lot of decisions and not include him in them, because I assumed he wouldn't want to be a part of them. I was used to making decisions by myself, and all of a sudden, I had someone in my life who wanted to make joint decisions, even about things I would categorize as being more "the wife's decision." Things like what kind of vacuum to buy or other furniture and decor decisions. Through time, especially that first year of marriage, I grew to learn that Ben is not like what I considered a typical guy, one who doesn't care about the house interior or other homemaking decisions. He is the opposite. Honestly, I found it annoying at first to talk through decisions, but now I've learned the merit in it. Ultimately, I want both of us to be content and happy with a decision, not just one of us. I've learned that marriage isn't about two roommates who get along and live separate lives in the same house. It's about joint decisions, commitment, and sometimes even staying up late at night until the issues are worked out.

Often I am still a maverick when it comes to my relationship with God. I jump to conclusions and don't go to him first. I put my wants and ideas first instead of focusing on God and what he says in his Word. I don't want to wait on God, but, rather, I want to expedite things in every way possible and maneuver my life around so that it pleases me. God did not make his people to be mavericks in this life. He's made us to be always and completely dependent on him for our bodies, our souls, our loved ones, and our eternities.

I guess you could say you know a fair amount about me. You know about my family, my husband, my friends, my job, my passions, my fears, and my sorrows. As you know, I am guilty of expecting God to follow my timing. You know I completed a 180 about waiting on God more to show me his patience, his timing, his love through others, and his strength. And you know that through this 180, God has shown me abundant grace.

My name is Stephanie Ihlen. I am still waiting.

A thousand times, thank you for taking the time to walk with me, talk with me, and listen to me. I am honored to share this 180 journey with you and can't wait to hear about yours! "Be joyful in hope, patient in affliction, faithful in prayer" (Romans 12:12).